PRAISE FOR *GOING DOWN TO THE RIVER*

"Doug Seegers has been a friend and inspiration since we first met, days before we began recording his debut album, *Going Down to the River*. This is his story. A good old-fashioned rising-from-the-ashes tale told—and lived—with grace and gratitude. Doug's story will inspire you too."

—Will Kimbrough

"When I met Doug Seegers in 1974, I knew we were connected. I didn't know what lay ahead for him, but I was touched by his huge talent and the cry of his soul. His story is a beautiful reminder of how God can change a heart and life when you least expect it, and then go on to touch others through you."

—Buddy Miller

"Doug Seegers's first-person account of homelessness and addiction stands as one of the greatest comeback stories in modern music. That the worst of it happened well before his much-deserved break-through as a sixty-three-year-old singer-songwriter says as much about spiritual resilience as it does undeniable talent."

—Rodney Crowell

GOING DOWN TO THE RIVER

GOING DOWN TO THE RIVER

A Homeless Musician, an Unforgettable Song,
and the Miraculous Encounter
That Changed a Life

DOUG SEEGERS

and Steve Eubanks

NELSON BOOKS

An Imprint of Thomas Nelson

Published in Nashville, Tennessee, by Nelson Books, an imprint of Thomas Nelson. Nelson Books and Thomas Nelson are registered trademarks of HarperCollins Christian Publishing, Inc.

Thomas Nelson titles may be purchased in bulk for educational, business, fund-raising, or sales promotional use. For information, please e-mail SpecialMarkets@ThomasNelson.com.

Unless otherwise noted, Scripture quotations are taken from the Holy Bible, New International Version®, NIV®. Copyright © 1973, 1978, 1984, 2011 by Biblica, Inc.™ Used by permission of Zondervan. All rights reserved worldwide. www.zondervan.com. The "NIV"and "New International Version" are trademarks registered in the United States Patent and Trademark Office by Biblica, Inc.™ Scripture quotations marked ESV are taken from are taken from the Holy Bible, New International Version®, NIV®. Copyright © 1973, 1978, 1984, 2011 by Biblica, Inc.™ Used by permission of Zondervan. All rights reserved worldwide. www.zondervan.com. The "NIV"and "New International Version" are trademarks registered in the United States Patent and Trademark Office by Biblica, Inc.™ Scripture quotations marked KJV are taken from the King James Version of the Bible, public domain.

Any Internet addresses, phone numbers, or company or product information printed in this book are offered as a resource and are not intended in any way to be or to imply an endorsement by Thomas Nelson, nor does Thomas Nelson vouch for the existence, content, or services of these sites, phone numbers, companies, or products beyond the life of this book.

Lyrics to the following are reprinted by permission of the author: "Going Down to the River," "Burning a Hole in My Pocket," "Angie's Song," "Memory Lane," and "Give It Away."

ISBN 978-0-7180-9658-0 (eBook)

Library of Congress Cataloging-in-Publication Data

Names: Seegers, Doug, author.
Title: Going down to the river: a homeless musician, an unforgettable song, and the miraculous encounter that changed a life / Doug Seegers.
Description: Nashville, Tennessee: Nelson Books, [2018] | Includes bibliographical references.
Identifiers: LCCN 2017023966 | ISBN 9780718095673
Subjects: LCSH: Seegers, Doug. | Country musicians—United States—Biography. | Homeless persons—United States—Biography.
Classification: LCC ML420.S446 A3 2018 | DDC 782.421642092 [B]—dc23 LC record available at https://lccn.loc.gov/2017023966

Printed in the United States of America

18 19 20 21 22 LSC 10 9 8 7 6 5 4 3 2 1

CONTENTS

CHAPTER 1

WHERE MIRACLES LIVE

Near as I can tell, when you look at the world and everybody in it, being homeless just in itself ain't a failing, moral or otherwise. I ought to know. Whether lying under a bridge in Tennessee, doing my best to stay warm and get a little shut-eye before the dawn parade of eighteen-wheelers rattles the highway overhead like tiny earthquakes, or on days like today when I'm ordering room service in one of the best hotels in Stockholm, I try to look at every day as a test. A few years ago, my test was to trust God as I was looking for a hot meal and some cardboard or a blanket to block the wind.

I can't say I was unhappy being homeless. In fact, it's the opposite. I didn't have any bills; didn't have anybody telling me what to do, where to go, what to wear, or how to speak; didn't have any responsibilities (or so I figured at the time); didn't have the weight of the world loading me down. I was out in nature, living each day free and easy. But I did have accountability. I was answerable to the Maker of all those trees I was sleeping under; responsible to the Creator of that water in the creek where I bathed and filled a cup to drink; accountable to the Giver of life, the Father of the ground I slept on more nights than not. I had a responsibility to live a life pleasing to him. Now my test is to keep him out front as I'm playing sold-out shows, selling records, signing autographs, and posing for pictures.

Because of where I've been, I know that it don't matter if you live in a palace or a box: Your standing with the Almighty doesn't change just because you get dinner out of a dumpster instead of having it delivered with a white napkin and a bunch of forks. Homelessness ain't noble, but it's not the worst of a man, either. What matters ain't where you live, it's how you live.

How I lived was rougher than the ground I slept on. The sinning I've done would make a hard man blush, just as the praying I've done—the begging to the Lord for strength and forgiveness—would cause that same man to cry like a little child. But on both sides of my life, being homeless never made me ashamed. I guess it's because poverty had been with me for as long as I'd had memory. Whether it was me and my brother rummaging through dumpsters looking for bicycle parts, or me throwing a thumb in the air and hitchhiking across the country, wherever I needed to go, I'd always lived in the corners. It's where I was comfortable—where I knew how to get along. Sometimes I had a place, an apartment or a house, especially when my kids were young. Other times I made do with a cot at a shelter, a tent in the woods, a jail cell and a jumpsuit, or a bedroll under the moon. Finding a place to bunk and a bite to eat every night was part of life's adventure, the tests I figured were all part of God's plan.

That kind of living's rough for people to look at. Folks sure had a hard time looking at me. Most of the time I didn't have much trouble getting by. I could always find a meal, either at a shelter or in a dumpster. Food's around if you know where to look. But when my fellow man avoided eye contact—when people stared out the windshield without so much as a blink, and me standing right next to 'em flying a cardboard flag that said, "Hungry, Any Little Bit Helps"—well, that'll put a hard, heavy weight on you. Make you think about life and what's really valued in a person. Ignoring ain't easy; it's just familiar. There's a rawness about a fella trotting to the other side of the road to avoid you, running away, and hoping it don't look too obvious. It'd be a shame to hear a man say, "Good morning" or "God bless" if there was any chance he might hit you up for some spare change or a dollar or two to get through the day.

Funny how the look of a man means so little, and yet so much. My clothes are better now, I guess, although the pantries and shelters always had fine things. Wearing a flannel shirt and jeans in Nashville is a sign that you're either homeless or a millionaire country music star with a mansion and a tour bus. You could be a rancher, a lawyer, a bootlegger—no telling. I've never been sure how people could spot a homeless person, at least from far enough away to avoid you. Yeah, I'd lost some

---

teeth by the end of it, and I ate a lot of my meals from places most folks wouldn't even touch. I drank water from my hands out of a creek, and sometimes my dinner plate was a tin pot on the ground. Showering wasn't always a daily thing, but my hair looked all right and I always had shoes. I wore my T-shirts right side out most of the time, and I didn't shuffle or yell at voices nobody else could hear like some of the poor souls down there. I guess it's just a feeling that drives folks away. As I've spent more time in the Bible, I think a lot about John the Baptist, long-haired, wearing camel hide, eating bugs and honey, hollering at crowds to repent. You reckon he'd go over in Nashville or New York today?

At least I had my guitar. There were a lot of times when that made all the difference. With a six-string in front of me, I wasn't looked at like a hobo, or a vagrant, or whatever down-and-dirty word you'd use to push your fellow man a notch or two below you. I was an attraction, a street artist. I was "bohemian," I heard more than once. A couple of chords into a song, and heads always turned. People would slow their walks or stop altogether and listen. Most would smile, maybe tap their toes. Some would eventually throw a few bucks into the case I had open with an "Out of Work" sign propped up inside it.

One time I was sitting on a bench near the bus stop, playing on the street, when a bunch of teenage girls came out of a restaurant at the corner. They were all talking at once and giggling the way girls do. Then they heard my song and just broke out dancing. It was a big, happy group. There wasn't a boy among them, so I changed it up and played something slow to see what they'd do. Well, they paired up and swayed to the beat without missing a step. Couple of them put together a little waltz, which was funny since I wasn't playing anything near that kind of music. When one of the moms came out, I told her how beautiful that scene was. The happiness of those girls, the innocence of them, it was hard not to see it without smiling. I told that mom how she should enjoy this time.

She smiled and nodded, assuming nothing bad out of me. Nothing at all. Without my guitar, that wouldn't have been the case. Put that thing away and I was worse than invisible; I was contagious. When it was just me with my hands in my pockets, people steered clear.

A buddy of mine named John from the streets in East Nashville puts old road maps in the windows of his Ford pickup so he can get some sleep during the day. John's rich in the homeless world because he has a vehicle and can get to a job so long as there's gas. He still eats out of dumpsters some, and he struggles with addiction and with losing time, and has trouble with memory, like so many of us. But he doesn't play or sing, so he doesn't have a draw, nothing to connect him with people. Music did that for me.

It's doing it still.

I think about those days on the streets with my guitar when people cheer at my shows, when they buy my records in a country I couldn't have found on a map just a few years ago. Who would have thought that a fella who'd been writing and singing country and Americana music for fifty years; a boy who grew up in Queens, New York, listening to bluegrass; a man who rambled in and out of homelessness in Nashville without selling a single record—who coulda believed that somebody like that would be one of the bestselling acts in Sweden in his midsixties? I never would have considered it. Yet, here we are.

The word *miracle* gets a lot of work nowadays. Too much, I think. A tree limb falls a few inches from your car and that's a miracle. A storm blows north, failing to upset your picnic, and you proclaim it a miracle. Your favorite sports team wins a game: miracle. You get a promotion: miracle. Your son or daughter gets accepted into a fancy school: a surefire, by-God-Almighty miracle if there ever was one. But a man in his darkest time puts down a needle, prays for strength, and gets hisownself together: somehow that doesn't count. A prostitute finds God, turns her life around, and gets a job at a local coffee shop: most people won't use the word *miracle* for that, and they won't say *angel* for the woman who hires her.

I've seen miracles because I know that man who used to carry a ragged tourniquet and dirty needle in his pocket. I know the young woman who used to work the streets, that girl who found forgiveness and the treasures of a new life. And I know the people who helped 'em. Not in the way you say you know somebody just because you've got a story that lines up with theirs—I know 'em by name. They were friends in my old life, and we're still friends in our new ones. I know a miracle when I see it, too, because I am one: a straight-up miracle of almighty God. He saved me to tell this story.

I still have some of the same clothes I had when I was sleeping and eating wherever I could. I wear the same T-shirts, some with the names of restaurants or car dealerships or radio stations printed on the front. They were giveaways, afterthoughts, which is sort of what people think of folks like me. My hats are nicer now. I've had a good many of my teeth fixed, but that can't be all of it. People stop and speak now. They ask me how things are going. They want to know when the new record's coming out, or when I'm heading back to Europe. People who knew me before—the people who never trotted to the other side of the road and who went out of the way to help me—they've told all their friends my story. There's a group of them, not groupies, at least not in America, but supporters and fans.

In Sweden, the crowds are unbelievable. The reception I get would go to most men's heads. If you look at the lives of many young people who find early success in music, you see just how bad it can be for you. Fame's a powerful drug. Too many musicians get wrapped up in the party. They end up flat broke or worse. I did it backward. I hit rock bottom before I got famous. For a long time, my success seemed overwhelming, and I cried almost every day when I thought about where I'd been and what was happening to me. 'Course, if I'd been a younger man and hadn't been where I've been, hadn't seen what I've seen, and done what I've done, it probably would have gotten to me too. All that cheering and people calling my name, the musicians who want to play with me, who want to sing my songs. It's still a high that I fight. Thankfully, success came late enough for me to know what it means, to know where the glory lies.

I've got a couple of suits I wear for shows sometimes, made for me by a fan, a sweet Swedish lady who wanted me to look my best. One's white with blue embroidery, trimmed out like what Hank Williams wore at the Opry. The other's reversed—blue with white embroidery. I still love Hank's words and how they touch people sixty years later. I also think about where and how he lived.

Hank always had a place: his mama's boardinghouse in Georgiana, Alabama, in the early days, and a home in Montgomery later. He was twenty-four when he wrote "I Saw the Light" in the back of a car coming home from a show.

By age twenty-nine Hank was dead.

I was sixty-three and living under a bridge when I saw the light and found God's way.

I know I won't ever turn 'em out like Hank, or have the Cadillacs or the houses. But I do know a couple of things: Our caskets will be the same size, and we'll both be held to account for how we used the gifts laid out in front of us. Tests will be graded for all. They surely will.

My story's not easy, or pretty, or quick. I look back on that younger man with thick, black hair, a bandana around his neck and a sparkle in his eyes. I want to drag him offa that street, kick him outta that crack house. I want to warn him never to take that first hit, never to taste that first drink, never to listen to that first little voice telling him, "Walk away—you don't owe them nothing" or "Go lay down awhile with that woman. It'll be good." I want to plead with him to never let the Devil into his mind, his heart, and his life. I want to read God's Word to him, out loud, as an older man should to a younger one. I want to let him know that without a seed there can be no harvest.

———

That ain't just a message for prosperity in this life; it's one of redemption for the next. It's one I wish I'd paid attention to a lot sooner. I want to get up behind that younger version of myownself, and push that boy onto the right and righteous path. But that wasn't the plan. All that hardness, all the hurt, it was for these last years—these successful days when I can show others what a real miracle looks like. It was so I could tell others that it's not too late. No matter how low you've gone, no matter what you've done, it's not too late.

It never is.

My healing ain't just spiritual. There's a physical healing that comes with walking the right road, although I'm still not the man I was before. When I was on the street, the drugs buggered up a good chunk of my brain. I forget a lot, and still have trouble piecing things together from my past. I was, to use a term from the seventies and eighties, a "burnout." I not only get confused about events from my time as a homeless person, but I sometimes have false memories. I recall certain things as plain as day. Problem is, they didn't happen. For many people, that kind of self-inflicted damage is permanent. Even after you've put down the crack pipe and cleaned up your life, certain damage doesn't heal. Part of my miracle is how God restored a good helping of my mind—not all of it, but a fair bit—as well as my body.

I do wish my memory were better. There are gaps. Big ones. Don't let anybody tell you that drugs don't cause permanent damage. They surely do. Things that I believe happened in a matter of days took place weeks and sometimes months and years apart. There's also some stuff I don't remember at all: terrible things—things I guess I blocked to keep from facing 'em. As I've pieced my story together, I've had to rely a good bit on other folks to fill in some holes. Parts have been painful. We spin things to puff ourselves up, all of us—sometimes for other people, but most of the time to convince ourownselves that we ain't as failed as the facts indicate. Mind-altering drugs don't help. They're as dangerous and deadly as a bad man with a gun. I oughta know. But it's important that I give it to you without flinching, or at least as much as I recollect, even with the help of others.

For the better part of a year after my last shot of whiskey or my final taste of an illegal drug, I couldn't remember the names of people I saw almost every day. I couldn't recall events that should've been branded into my memory. Some people can't conceive of being homeless, because their minds work different than the person on the street. I've been both places, and, as far as my thinking goes, I still hover somewhere between the two.

The power of prayer cannot be denied. Jesus healed the blind, the deaf, the crippled. He healed people so eaten up with leprosy that their skin was falling away like leaves from a dying tree. He healed those folks that others wouldn't touch, wouldn't look at. He ran to the ones everyone else pretended didn't exist. He's doing it still.

When I think about the men who wrote the Gospels, men who followed Jesus and who talked to folks who were there with him every day, I always smile and shake my head at what they said about theirownselves. Not a one of 'em told the story like they were the big shot. Nobody said, "Yeah, those others didn't believe he'd come back from the dead, but I surely did." Not a single one among 'em said, "The rest of 'em was terrified when he appeared in front of us, but I wasn't scared." Nobody who was there said, "Yeah, everybody else slid back in the crowd, but I tried to stand up for him against the Romans." They all, every one of 'em, told it like it happened: the dark story of weak men saved by a grace not a one of 'em deserved.

Live my story with me. Marvel at the grace I didn't deserve. Don't look away. Don't run to the other side of the road or pretend you don't see me. Open your eyes. Open your heart.

Witness a miracle.

CHAPTER 2

SEEDS

I never met my dad's family. Don't know the first thing about 'em, which has never really bothered me other than not being able to pass anything on beyond the name. It's kind of awkward when kids ask about your grandparents or where your folks are from and you don't have the first, foggiest notion. That'll leave you off-kilter if you let it, especially when you know the kids asking are at that age where family questions ain't out of curiosity. They need to find something in their own selves, something they can latch onto like a dock cleat—something to keep them from drifting too far out. Something to make 'em feel real.

Unfortunately, I can't numb you with a list of great-great-great-grandparents or give any real family history at all. I don't even know where my dad grew up; Midwest somewhere, I think, although I might have dreamed that. Nobody ever said, and I never asked. Mom used to have a photo of him that was taken somewhere in Nashville during one of his far-flung road trips—there seemed to be a good many of those—but that picture's been gone so many years it's a wonder I remember it. John Harvey Seegers wasn't from Tennessee or anywhere in the South. I don't remember much about him, but I'd have remembered a Southern accent, something I've grown to love. The man who first married my mom didn't have that note of the South in him, or anything else that I admired.

'Course, Mom didn't see the bad in him in the beginning. She was a kid with teenage memories of World War II, and the hard times before it. Her folks, my grandparents, Muriel and Giuliano Ahrens (everybody called Grandpa "Googie"), sheltered her from the worst: neighbors starving in the Depression, folks giving up their children because they couldn't feed them, people living in lean-tos or loading everything they owned into pickup trucks and heading out for parts unknown. Even with protective parents, nobody got out of that time unscarred. Mom felt the worry. How could you not? You couldn't walk more than a couple of blocks in New York without running up on a soup line.

Homelessness, even though that word didn't exist at the time, was a part of everybody's life. If you hadn't lost it all, you knew somebody who had. Folks in that time weren't equipped to deal with it any better than people are today. There wasn't a "safety net," so people made up new words like *hobo* for the ones who were more than willing to work but who had to hop a freight train to get to the jobsites, catch as they could. Men rode the rails and slept in barns and culverts back then. Many of 'em were boys under the age of nineteen, some put out by their folks because there wasn't enough food for everybody.

Mom saw them, and she saw how they were treated. During the war, she also caught glances of mothers shaking and wailing as their knuckles turned white holding telegrams from the Department of War. That sort of thing sticks to you. Stains you like hot grease.

It's no wonder my grandparents beat a trail out of town as soon as the war was over. They weren't alone. I read somewhere that the stampede out of the city in the late 1940s was like uprooting and moving entire states. Most didn't go far. They crossed the bridge and turned the potato fields and hickory forests of Long Island into healthy-sized towns, creating another word: *suburb*.

From what I gather, times got good then. Boys who'd been living in one-room basement apartments with six or seven siblings, shank to flank, before the war, came back, married, and headed to Levittown or Rockaway. They got jobs and bought brand-spanking-new houses that they filled with electric clothes dryers and dishwashers. And they bought cars: sleek and shiny ones with back seats the size of church pews. My uncle Ben, who drove a truck for Getty Oil, customized cars as a hobby. He tore down and bored out more engines than I could count, but that wasn't unusual back in that time. Everybody wanted a new ride with a rumbling Detroit engine and a grille the size of a surfboard. A year or two into a good job and you could get it. And you could have the whole world beamed into your living room through a new RCA television. There were Howard Johnson restaurants and drive-in movie theaters, bars, coffee shops, dance halls, and night clubs, all new, popping up as fast as the houses in Hicksville.

I try to think about what it must have been like. Coming out of the Depression with homelessness hanging over every family, it must have been like a storm had lifted. As bad as things got torn up, people were still happy to be alive and see the sunshine. That was just the right time and place and the perfect state of mind for a smiling, drifting musician like my dad, John Harvey Seegers, to sweep up an innocent girl like Marilyn Ahrens.

Dad fancied himself a music rebel, something between Les Paul and Lefty Frizzell, open collars and growling boogie-woogie. Sometimes he'd sing Frizzell in the house: *"If you got the money, honey, I got the time."* Dad called himself Johnny Rivers onstage, long before that name got picked up by a kid from Baton Rouge who had some hits in the sixties, including "Secret Agent Man" and "Poor Side of Town." That Johnny Rivers, the one who became famous, was ten years old when John Harvey tried to play the big time as Johnny Rivers and the Rest Tones.

There wasn't a lot Mom couldn't sing, although she mostly stuck to gospel and bluegrass. When it came to church music, her voice soared like the heavenly host. She also played bass fiddle and would occasionally sit in with Dad's band. I don't know if he was jealous of her, or insecure, but I know Mom was the better musician. Her whole family had music in 'em. They learned to play instruments like other people learned to walk and talk, and they heard rhythms and harmonies that other people missed. Walk down the street with a crowd of folks, and my grandma Ahrens would find a downbeat and write a song on the fly. If Googie or Mom were with her, they'd pick up and harmonize before we got to the end of the block. It had to gnaw at Dad, knowing that the woman he was seeing could make beautiful music sound so simple.

They were married—I don't know a thing about when or where—and they had my older brother, Dave, pretty quick. I came two years after Dave, in 1952, by which time things were already rocky at home. Dad wanted to cut hit records, drive big cars, and play sold-out shows. Johnny Rivers and the Rest Tones played whatever juke joints they could find. Music was changing. Crooners were the thing: Tony Bennett, Nat King Cole, Perry Como, Frank Sinatra, and women like Rosemary Clooney, Patti Page, and Dinah Shore. Even Hank Williams, who had all his hits in that same time, was considered a regional star. It wasn't till he was dead that Hank's work got the widespread attention it deserved.

Dad wasn't any of that. He was a honky-tonker, nothing more. He'd slick his hair back and give half-snarl smiles to whatever young things in tight sweaters happened to sidle up to the stage, and he thought he was hot stuff. Every extra penny went to equipment or a fancy new shirt. He had to have a car to get to the shows, a big showboat one that people would notice the second it rolled up. There were shiny shoes, fancy guitar straps, and a hat or two. He had to have it all while Mom looked after two babies in a small, second-floor apartment in Far Rockaway, Queens, right above a market where Mom would wander the aisles, stretching a grocery dollar so far it almost snapped.

Young-boy memories slip just out of reach for old men. Sometimes it's hard to recollect if a thing really happened, or if your brain just put it there because you wanted it to be true. I do know that my grandparents did their best. Before I turned five, my grandpa Googie got me away from my feuding folks and walked me down to a local tavern. There weren't strict rules about kids in bars in those days. The place smelled like ocean sweat, unfiltered cigarettes, fried chicken, and brown liquor. Loud voices ran through a little boy like lightning.

"Googie brought his grandson."

"Hey, look at the kid."

"What's he drinking, Googie?" Laughter all around. Grandpa was a big hit, and so was I. He lifted me onto the bar and got everybody's attention.

"Listen up. My grandson Doug here's gonna entertain you." We'd rehearsed this part, but being there, up so high with so many big faces staring at me, the room so dark it could have gone on forever, a sea of blackness filled with grown-up sounds and smells, I started to shake with fear. I took my time and Grandpa counted the beat, "One, two, three, four . . ." I immediately belted out "Hound Dog," the Big Mama Thornton song Elvis had just covered. *You ain't nothin' but a hound dog / cryin' all the time.* I squinted as I sang, and I did my best to jiggle. The crowd ate it up. They cheered, and clapped, and stood, and hooted. Grandpa held up my hand like a prizefighter. Just like that, I had my first real memory. That it came in a smoky room with alcohol and music, well, that pretty much sums up a big chunk of my life.

———

Fact is, my grandparents filled a lot of holes for us. My grandma Muriel would help us make Kool-Aid, pouring the powder into the wide-mouth pitcher and stirring it with a wooden spoon that looked the size of an oar to a little boy. I'd jump up and down as the granules swirled and danced until the water turned red. It was like some magic brew. Me and Dave drank our fill and then sold Dixie Cups of it on the corner for a nickel, or a dime on the hottest days. Some people would make a big deal, complaining about the price—"A dime for that small cup? That's highway robbery!"—but they'd always pay, hiding smiles as best they could. Dave got good at comebacks.

"Hot as it is, we ought to charge a quarter," he'd say.

I kept quiet, happy to have any money at all. I rubbed those dimes together like I thought it'd make 'em multiply. All I could think about was buying bicycles and ice cream. After an afternoon in the hot sun, Mom and Grandma would count the money for us when we came inside. They'd put it in a mason jar on the shelf beside the sink.

"When you sell a little more, we'll go to the candy store," Grandma would say. And, good to her word, we'd go, me and Dave with Grandma or Grandpa. We mostly bought hard candy. Taffy and chocolate were too expensive, and I hadn't built up a

———

taste for licorice. But those hard candies looked like diamonds. It felt really good to spend my own money on 'em.

After a time or two, the regulars in our neighborhood weren't as interested in parting with a dime for a tiny cup of Kool-Aid. Dave got restless. He was older and didn't want to spend his afternoons with me. He started naming the cars that passed on the street, learning the makes and models. He got to the point where he could tell the engines by the sound: a 1958 Buick Limited with an overhead V8; the '54 Eldorado, 5.4-liter, 230 horsepower; the '57 Chevy, the one every slick-haired, nineteen-year-old kid tried to turn into a dragster. My uncle Ben, who had a '57 Chevy, candy-apple red with an engine that sounded like a fighter jet, helped Dave learn the ins and outs of cars. It never occurred to either of us that these were things a father shoulda been doing with his boys. None of those best memories include Dad. Googie and Uncle Ben were the men in our lives at that time. That was all we knew, so it was fine with us.

I couldn't have cared less about cars, though I did learn enough about engines to fix up a clunker later in life when I needed a ride. The only thing in them that really interested me at the time was the radio. When people drove by with open windows, I'd strain to hear a bar or two of whatever song was playing: the Fleetwoods, Frankie Avalon, Ritchie Valens, Paul Anka, *"I'm just a lonely boy / lonely and blue."* I'd hum and sing until the car turned the corner and the last note drifted away. Then I'd listen for the next one.

Mom took us to her parents' house a lot more than most

mothers on our block. I figured we were lucky. Mom was happy around her folks. You could see her change. Her shoulders dropped and her face perked up. Why that happened was a mystery to young boys, but we were happy with her. Some of my best memories are of the practical jokes Mom would pull on Grandpa.

Once, she stopped at the dime store and bought some of that awful rubber vomit, the gag stuff that looked real when you put it on the floor. At Grandma's dinner table, when Grandpa went to the fridge, Mom gagged and coughed, lurched forward, and put that rubber vomit on the floor. Grandpa ran over and put his arm on her back.

"Oh, no!" he shouted. "What's wrong, honey?"

Mom reached down and picked up the prop, and doubled over again, this time laughing. Googie didn't find that too funny right off, but he joined in with us cackling soon enough.

Seems like we were always there around events and holidays. Mom and my grandmother always made our Halloween costumes. Dave would be a cowboy and I'd go as a Chinese monk, complete with a hat, gown, and painted-on Fu Manchu mustache. Grandma would put makeup around my eyes to make 'em look Asian, just the sort of thing that'd send folks into sputtering fits nowadays. We didn't think twice about it. Mom wasn't insulting the Chinese with my outfit any more than she was swiping at cowboys with Dave's, or taking a stab at witches with her own.

Mom had the best witch costume I'd ever seen, with a pointy hat that looked like it went up forever. She'd sing as we walked, and she'd encourage other kids to join in. Like the Pied Piper, it didn't take her long to draw a crowd. Music attracted people to us. It always had and always would. Mom would sing when we went to the market without enough money for weekly rations. She'd sing until people walking down the street raised their heads and smiled. No matter what was happening in our lives, Mom's music washed away our troubles, at least for a while.

My father was absent from all these memories. There are flickers—a time here and there when we were all together—but most of my boyhood was with my brother, mother, grandparents, uncle, and cousins. Those few times Dad made an impression, it wasn't a great one. He'd blow in late after a show, long after Dave and I were tucked into our bunk beds, with just enough whiskey breath to jolt us awake. He'd bounce into our room, fired up and ready to talk about the parts of his night that puffed him up. Mom would run in behind him, shushing, trying to get him out before he wound us up to the ceiling.

"Why would you do this?"

"Because they're my boys. Why would you try to get between a man and his sons?"

"Because they have school. Because it's late." Because. Because. Because. Those nights always ended the same.

The more Dad veered into his bad-boy, rockabilly ego, the more Mom wandered back to the simpler things: homemade meals, rocking chairs, refinishing old wood, and the mandolin trills of Bill Monroe. On quiet afternoons, she'd put on the records she loved: Lester Flat and Earl Scruggs, or the Osborne Brothers, especially Bobby Osborne, who always made her smile. Her music skewed toward roots, with pain and faith at the core. Despite talent that would stop any man in his tracks, after a while she quit playing bass in public. Her music stayed in the family and at church. Looking back, I know that decision was for us. She might not have thought about it, but a good mother can sense when bad things creep up on her boys. Dad's honky-tonking fit the bill. So Mom's instincts took over, and she moved toward the stable things in life: home, family, and church. Her music struck those same chords.

I remember one night at my grandparents' place when Dad blew in like a storm and called us all down to the small television in the den. When the screen glowed to life, I recognized Ed Sullivan, the guy with the show that had monkeys and men juggling plates. I'd always figured Mr. Sullivan suffered from some malady or other that made him stand that way. He introduced the Everly Brothers, and Dad shouted, "That's them! That's them! Now, listen." The room filled with harmonies: "*Wake up little . . .*" Grandma nodded to the beat, and Mom patted her leg as she broke into the most genuine smile I could remember. I was too young to know about adult troubles, but I knew love when I felt it. That night Ed Sullivan and the Everlys filled our family with a warm goodness.

Those feelings weren't around long or often, though. Johnny Rivers and the Rest Tones cut one record, then another, but they went nowhere. Bitterness festered up in Dad like a boil. He made excuses. Nobody would promote him. The record didn't get any radio play because all the DJs got kickbacks. He didn't have a manager to book bigger gigs. Nobody took the time to listen. On and on he'd go, getting sadder and meaner by the minute.

Our family seemed to be left out of all the booming success we saw around us. Jobs were good in the fifties. Every day saw a new plant opening and a new product coming out, but none of it seemed to be for us. A million people went to work in the aviation and defense industries in Nassau and Suffolk counties. Thousands of jobs at the Brookhaven National Laboratory got gobbled up by men willing to work. If you couldn't get on in those plants, you could find a job building them. Construction was everywhere. If you knew how to swing a hammer or dig a hole you could get a good job in New York. Still, Mom scrimped and saved, just as her family had done in the Depression. Dad stayed out late and lived the life of a starving musician, doing Lord knows what with bandmates and fans—things that didn't match up with being a married father of two. We were more than a burden to him; we were the perfect excuse. A wife and kids hold an artist back. When you're looking for an excuse, you go with what's convenient, and we were right there.

In his mind, it was our fault—me and Mom and Dave—that he couldn't break out of Long Island bars or the Ithaca VFW Hall. Without the ball and chain of a wife and kids, he'd surely have gold records hanging on the walls of his big ol' house with a pool out back. Without a family to feed, he'd have been free to travel the country and be discovered; he'd have found his own Colonel Tom Parker; he'd have been on television like Elvis and the Everlys.

Mom tried to hide the turmoil from us, but boys sense

things in their mothers. I was especially sensitive. I didn't know why she was low, but I wanted to set things right, so I'd hug and pat her leg while singing one of her favorite songs, "Roll Muddy River, Roll On." She'd smile and rub my hair, but the sadness never left her eyes.

On my eighth birthday, Mom took me five blocks uptown to the nearest pawnshop. I'd been begging her for a while, but I wasn't sure if I'd ever get my wish, so it was a big thrill when she said I could choose one of the dusty, out-of-tune guitars hanging on the wall. I might as well have been in Santa's workshop.

"Just make sure the neck's not warped," Mom said. "Need to find one with a good saddle and nut. That chip on the head-stock won't hurt a thing. But we gotta make sure the bridge pins and machine heads hold. Strings are expensive. We need 'em to last."

Dad would've been better suited for this, especially with me showing an interest in following in his footsteps, but he couldn't make it. Late night. Headache. Somehow, at the ripe old age of eight, I missed the message there. I was too busy plucking every string, strumming the chords Mom had taught me on the spot. When we decided on one, Mom took several deep breaths as she dug the money out of her purse. I have no idea how much she paid, but it sure didn't cost what it was worth. Not to me.

That guitar turned out to be more than a prize possession or a priceless gift from a loving mother; it was a shield. When I picked it up, as I did first thing in the morning, I felt like I went into my own world, a place where none of the harsh talk and bad words affected me. Most of the time I didn't put it down until I was too tired to stay upright, and sometimes I didn't drop it then. More than once I fell asleep with that old guitar on my chest and woke up holding the neck. Mom made me put it down to eat, but that was the only time I wasn't picking it when I was home and awake.

I played what songs I could make out from the radio: *"Blue moon, keep on shining bright."* I stretched out my hand to reach the bar chords and picked at the calluses that formed on my fingertips, proud of myself when they stopped hurting. I hummed what songs I wasn't quite ready to sing. Kids wall theirownselves off from hurt, most of the time without knowing they're doing it. That pawnshop box wrapped me up and kept me safe while my parents feuded. It didn't fend off all the hurt, but it sure helped.

At the time, I didn't know what perfect pitch was, but Grandma had it. She was the best musician in the family. I'd walk around with that guitar trying to find chords and Grandma would say, "Hum it." I would, and she'd tell me the notes and where to find them on the fret board. When the Beatles first came out, Grandma was their biggest fan. She would call me to the radio every time one of their songs came on.

"Listen to that harmony," she'd say. "See how tight they got it? Boys have worked real hard to make it sound that easy. The easier something sounds, the harder they've worked at it."

I always remembered that, even when I didn't live it.

I worked like crazy on that old guitar. It held another little bit of magic; that darned instrument somehow attracted my dad to me. It didn't matter if I was doing pick drills or fumbling through a song, the times that Dad was around, he'd inch a little closer to me when I played. Most times he stayed quiet, but I could tell he was listening. I went at it hard when I knew he was paying attention. Then one evening he said, "I'll make you a deal, Bub. You learn how to play 'Guitar Boogie' by the Drifting Cowboys and I'll buy you a new guitar."

He might as well have told me he'd fly me to the moon. A new guitar in our house was akin to telling a teenaged boy he could have a new Corvette. Poor families didn't have new things. Mom always made sure we had what we needed, even though it meant making her own clothes and mending ours till they were threadbare. Almost everything we had was second-hand. A new guitar, that was like the dream at the end of the rainbow.

Dad had a bunch of Hank Williams records stacked up, so I listened to that song and picked out the chords. Then I worked on it night and day, passing out many a late evening with the strap still on my shoulder. But Dad was gone before I learned it.

I wish that memory hadn't stuck with me the way it did.

———

We came to the kitchen that morning as we always did, shuffling and rubbing our eyes, anticipating the bowl of cereal in our future. When I saw Mom, I didn't know what had changed, but dread washed over me. I wasn't old enough to run through all the possible things that could've made her look so beat down, so lost, almost ghostly the way her shoulders hung.

———

"Dad's gone," she said as matter-of-factly as you can say something like that to young boys. Her voice rattled like a glass about to break. At first, I didn't think twice about Dad being gone. The band traveled sometimes. It wasn't unusual for him not to be there. That time of the morning, me and Dave would have thought something was wrong if he had joined us. Even when he was in the apartment, he was never up that early.

That's when Mom told us the rest of it. He wasn't gone for a day or two. He was gone from the family. Gone for good. He'd left us. He wanted to move on, start a new life somewhere else, with someone else. He had taken up with a groupie and intended to marry her, or so Mom guessed. He wouldn't be around to watch *Bonanza* or *Wagon Train* with us, wouldn't be there to add a tenor harmony when Mom broke out a hymn, wouldn't be there to hear me learn "Guitar Boogie," or any other song. Life would be different. Dad had tossed us aside.

Dave took it the hardest. He sat in his bed a lot, rocking back and forth with his knees pulled up to his chest, silent except for the heavy breathing, like a bull about to charge. I felt a kind of rage I didn't understand—not the tantrum kind kids have when they don't get their way, but a deep, hard hate that I let fester without saying much of anything. Abandonment doesn't hit a kid all at once. God builds walls for little ones. You don't realize how awful something is until you look back on it, and there are few things worse for a young boy than a dad walking away.

For the first year or two after, John Harvey came to visit us once a month. He'd take us out for a burger or a Coke. In the very beginning I looked forward to it, though I had mixed feelings because I knew he'd caused Mom to be sad all the time and sent Dave into a shell. After a few months, I would've rather gone to the doctor for a shot. Dave finally refused to go. I remember Dad showing up once in a big, purple Lincoln that looked long as a train car. I'm sure it had cost enough to feed us for a year. I didn't draw the line between him buying that car and Mom's soup getting thinner by the week, or the fact that the powdered milk was getting sugary and the bread stale, but before I was ten I knew what it meant when somebody tried too hard to be a big shot. Those visits didn't last long. Pretty quick Dad faded away like a bad smell. We never saw or heard from him again.

Mom moved into subsidized housing in the bad part of Babylon, near enough to Grandma and Grandpa to get some help if we needed it. Nights were still loud, but the noise was outside the apartment instead of inside. The people next door hollered at one another so much I figured they had to be deaf. Somebody was always fighting outside—a guy yelling at a girl, the girl yelling back, screaming, tires squealing, cussing that'll always perk up a young boy's ears, and finally, tears. That show played outside my window almost every night. There were a lot of boys like me and Dave in that part of town—kids with no money and no dad around, kids roaming the streets looking for some purpose, some bond, some connection to something.

We went on welfare, which had a lot more shame to it back then than it does now, or at least it did with Mom. I'd go to the welfare office with her as she filled out the forms. Even a young boy could see judgment in the eyes of the workers there.

"When did your husband leave?"

"How many children?"

"Have you tried to find work?"

Mom's shoulders sagged a little more with each trip. Before long, I stopped going with her.

Grandpa realized that I needed something to keep me busy, so he and Dave helped me find enough bicycle parts in the dumpster to piece together a decent ride. We spliced together some long handlebars and made grips out of duct tape. We found wheels that fit the frame, but the chain we found was way too long. Dave said he knew how to take links out of it, but he needed Grandpa's help. Shrinking that chain to size was slow work; each little rivet had to be removed without tearing up the whole thing. Then, once it was shortened, we had to connect the ends again and grease it up so the chain rode around the gear. I loved seeing garbage changed into something useful and beautiful.

In my case, the bike was also a means to a job. I got a paper route. I would get up every morning before five o'clock and hit the road, delivering 120 copies of the *Long Island Press* to neighbors. The spokes of my wheels would flip baseball cards that I'd put in the bike frame, and I'd hum to the rhythm of those clicks and clacks. I made two cents a paper and got a dollar at Christmas from almost everybody on the route. It felt good having money of my own, but a payday didn't fill the emptiness that I couldn't explain.

Pretty soon I parked my bike, put down my guitar, and picked up a brick. As silly as it sounds now, I joined as much of a gang as nine-to-thirteen-year-old boys could piece together back then. We hung out on street corners, cussed, and got into whatever other trouble we could find. Occasionally somebody'd snatch cigarettes from an adult or shoplift them from the local market. We'd all light up, puffing away and propping up on one hip like James Dean. I got good at holding a cigarette between my fingers and blowing smoke rings into the sky, a trick that took some practice and more than a few coughing fits to get right.

Sometimes me and the boys would play handball in the alleys or shoot dice behind one of the shops. If somebody got a marker or some paint, we'd put graffiti on a dumpster or the back walls of a building, usually a bad word or something that a boy that age would think was cool. This was long before gangs "tagged" anything. We were just fool kids feeling our way through that stage of life. I also taught a good many of my gang buddies how to sing harmonies: *"There goes my baby."* We must have been something out on those street corners, doing our best to look tough while we sang "The Lion Sleeps Tonight" and talked about how Dick Tracy was going to get Blockhead next time.

I would always go home at night, at first because I was afraid Mom would send a search party out for me. Then I hustled home because I was afraid she wouldn't.

Mom had always loved the grain of wood. Every apartment we lived in, she'd strip the paint off the floors and molding, taking the wood back to natural. More than once, I came home late from being out with my gang to find Mom on her knees, sanding away, her hands bleeding, her face a mask of red splotches and sweat. For a good while she asked me every night where I'd been. When those questions stopped, I started getting into trouble.

Once, we broke into a sporting goods store. There were bows and arrows in the windows. Me and my gang brothers wanted 'em, but didn't have enough money between us to buy a six-ounce soda. So one of the boys, I can't remember which one, grabbed a rock and said we should break in and take 'em. We were big dogs. This was our block. We ran things here. Who was going to stop us? I don't remember anybody objecting until that glass broke like a gunshot. A couple of gang members ran away immediately. The rest of us poured into that store with thievery on our minds and malice in our hearts. It was a hot rush for me. In a flash, I envisioned us taking those bows and arrows and holding up shops and taverns up and down the shoreline. We'd be the Hole-in-the-Wall Gang, and I'd be the Sundance Kid, pointing arrows at rich people and telling 'em to give us their money. We'd get across the bridge into the city and raid a few restaurants and stores there, escaping back to Babylon where no one could find us. Real gangsters.

Those thoughts vanished as quick as they'd come, because the police rolled up in what seemed like seconds. One of the kids inside the store tried to run. He made it about fifteen feet before being grabbed by the scruff of the neck and hauled back to the cruiser. Blue and red lights hit us like switches, and we were surrounded by men who looked like giants. My thoughts went from being a Wild West outlaw to wondering what jail we'd be in. On the street corner we'd talked about Rikers Island. Some of the boys said they'd been there to see relatives. The way they said it made me believe 'em. The way the cops were talking that night, I believed that was where we were headed.

When the cruiser pulled up in front of our apartment, all the neighbors stuck their heads out like groundhogs. Cops came as often as the mailman in our neighborhood, usually to haul off somebody who'd had too much hooch and gotten into a fight. Routine or not, it was a show, one that usually included a wife or girlfriend cussing at a cop and wailing like a spanked baby. That night the neighbors were surprised when the officer knocked on Mom's door.

"What'd she do?"

"Ain't her old man gone?"

I stood off to the side while Mom talked to the cops in voices barely above a whisper. I could pick up the tone, though. The cops were getting after Mom some, and she was a minute away from tears. Words like *abandoned* came up, followed by more serious whispers.

That night, after the lights went out, the cops drove away and the neighborhood quieted down, I heard Mom talking in her room. Nobody else was in the apartment, so I slipped down the hall and peeked in the door. She was on her knees with elbows on the bed, her head bowed. I'd seen Mom pray in church before, and I knew kids were supposed to say their prayers at night, but I figured, beyond saying grace over dinner, grown-ups didn't pray at home, especially out loud—especially alone in their rooms. That memory would come back many times over the years.

———

My venture into burglary jolted Mom into the reality that her boys needed some male guidance. Uncle Ben started coming over more. He put pinwheels on my bike and would listen to whatever songs I'd learned on the guitar. Ben played the banjo and would pick with me sometimes. "Orange Blossom Special" was his favorite. He could run off to the races on that one.

Grandpa would drive us out to Ben's house in Central Islip. His place was adjacent to a good stretch of county land, so it was like visiting the country. Ben even bought a horse for his stepson, Neal, who was my age. Me and Neal would ride that horse to a farm on the other side of the county land where a black bull grazed. The horse would stop and shake his head as the bull sized us up. The animals seemed to come to an understanding. The bull could gore us and leave us for dead. The horse was fast and free and could be gone in a second. We boys supposedly had dominion over all creatures, but we could have been thrown to the ground and stomped like bugs at any second, something we sensed more than knew. We were at peace with it. I loved those times.

Back home, our grandparents and Mom would take us to the beach as often as they could. Mom would give us sifters, and me and Dave would dig in the sand looking for coins. The real treat was finding a watch, or ring, anything that might have fallen from the pockets of those in less need. I would get lost in my own world out there, the sun knocking on my back, sand sliding through that sifter, and me sure that a treasure was one scoop away. The ocean always provided a good backbeat, and

I'd sing whatever melodies matched the rhythm of the waves. Sometimes I'd write songs about finding a gold coin in the sand, or running up on a genie in a bottle.

I barely noticed that Mom was dating again. It was the milkman, a good fella, but not somebody who warmed up to me and Dave. It wouldn't have helped if he'd taken us to every Mets game or treated us like long-lost prodigal sons. The Seegers boys had a hard wall between us and any man who tried to get too close. Scars harden, and we'd been cut deep. We knew what could happen if you let a man into your life. Just about the time you thought he'd be there to help you, to show you how to talk to a girl when the time came, teach you how to grill meat, or how to come to an agreement with a man about a job—just about the time you needed a man to get in your face about letting your temper get away, or lead by example by working hard and doing right—why, that man, whoever he was, just might take off in the middle of the night never to be seen again. That was not something me and Dave could handle again. So I played with stray dogs in the neighborhood and picked my guitar, learning to sing and play: *Up a lazy river by the old mill run / Lazy river in the noon day sun.*

Mom always told me not to take the music too serious. "Study and do your homework," she'd say. "Please don't think about playing that guitar for a living." 'Course, I thought of nothing else. Every day until I turned eighteen, I dreamed of being onstage, wooing a crowd with my songs. I was too young to understand that every chord I struck was a pinprick to Mom's heart. Fact is, I wouldn't know it until it was too late.

———

I played a Christmas show in Port Jefferson, New York, not too long ago. After it was over, I don't know why, but I headed south, unplanned, until I was standing outside the white clapboard and arched windows of the United Methodist Church of Babylon, the place my mom and grandma lit ablaze with gospel music. More than once their voices brought tears to the hardest men's eyes. Being a young boy, I didn't pay attention. I just remember my mom feeding us and dressing us up for Sunday school. I remember the backs of the pews being soft and the seats hard, wondering why somebody didn't switch that up. I remember singing too. Swaying, tapping my little feet as the music minister waved his arms.

God plants seeds in children. I really believe that. At the time, we're no more aware of it than the earth around a fallen acorn knows it'll someday spawn a yawning oak. But God protects memories and feelings in a child, like those that came back to me from that little white church.

Certain things stick with you for life, events you can always recall like they happened yesterday because of how they made you feel. Sunday mornings in that church, my mother wearing a robe in the choir loft like an angel, turning her face up, closing her eyes like God was shining on her through the ceiling, giving her answers to questions I was too young to hear—that feeling stays with me to this day.

I'd never once blame my troubles on my dad. A man's responsible for hisownself. The things I did are mine. I'll answer for 'em. But I'll say this: boys need men around—maybe not in the house every day, but around—watching, coaching, setting an example. I waited until my kids were teenagers before I moved to Nashville. I sat down with 'em and asked 'em if they were okay with me leaving. What I didn't realize at the time was how much my own leaving would hurt 'em, especially my son, Jacob. I didn't abandon 'em when they were tiny, although I did leave their mom when they were near babies. But I walked away from Jacob at exactly the wrong time. It pains me to think about that. I was not a great parent. Far from it. My blunders harmed my kids too. There's special, hot feelings sons have for the men that throw them out like dirty rags. That's a deep, dark hole for a little boy to climb out of. I admire those that do.

I was an old man before I understood that the forgiveness and love we're commanded to lay onto those who slight us, who hurt us in ways we can't put into words, are not for them. They're for us. Hate's a heavy thing, one you don't realize is weighing you down until you take it off and forgive the ones who've wronged you, whether they're around to receive that forgiveness or not. One of the last things Jesus said, hanging on the cross, was, "Forgive them, Father. They don't know what they're doing" (Luke 23:34, paraphrase).

That's tough teaching, but it's the center of everything faith holds as true. We don't know what we're doing half the time. You convince yourself that you can leave your wife and the kids won't be that tore up. They're young. They'll adapt. You'll still be there for 'em. Quality time. Every weekend. Won't miss. Dinner once a week. Why, that's more than you saw 'em when you were married. It'll be better for 'em, because you'll be happy. Those are the worst kinds of lies, because they're the ones you convince yourself are true, even when you know better. Yet you wonder why the kids hold those hot, hurt feelings for you, ones that they can't seem to let go, even into adulthood.

We all have someone we need to forgive, a person who don't deserve it, who hasn't asked for it, and who probably won't accept it if they're right in front of you when you do it. But we all need forgiveness too. In a lot of cases, we're the people who don't know it. More times than not, we're the ones who don't deserve it.

I sure wish I'd learned that lesson early in life. But my path was different, and not for the better.

CHAPTER 3

A TORCH IN MY SOUL

Mom remarried. Brian Dullahane was a hard worker, an early riser who took being a milkman deadly serious. He was also a navy veteran who didn't care much for long hair and rock and roll, all of which put him at odds with me and Dave from the start. Not that Brian, who we called Dad after a short while, didn't try.

Uncle Ben convinced Brian to get Mom and us farther away from the city, out of the projects and the problems that fell on poor people like a dirty rain. So he bought a small house on West Crest Avenue in West Islip, Suffolk County, New York, the first house we'd ever had. Just like that, we plopped into the middle class, which, according to every advertisement or television show I'd ever seen, should have cheered us boys right up. It didn't work out that way. Dave barely made it through school, spending most of his time under the hood of various cars. I surrounded myself with as many records as I could stack, touching the needle to the vinyl and bobbing my head to the beats.

The only thing our original dad left us was his record collection, a big stack of seventy-eights in onion-sheet wrappers: artists like Hank Williams, Johnny Cash, Tennessee Ernie Ford, Chet Atkins, Merle Haggard, Buck Owens, and Elvis. I dove headfirst into all of 'em, lifting the arm of the record player after every bar and placing it back a rib or two to listen again. That's how you replayed songs in the vinyl days. I did that hour after hour with my guitar in front of me. Soon I could play each song. That was how I really learned the guitar. I could strum my way through the hymnal, but before I spent time with those records, I wasn't really playing. Like everybody learning something new, I was slow at first. Frustration got me more'n once. Mom and my grandmother continued to help me with chords. I'd get a bar or two in, maybe a phrase, and then I'd hesitate and lose time. I'd fumble through a transition and stop singing until I got the notes right. I wondered why something I wanted so much took so long. Then, each time I'd get through a song without stopping or hesitating, I felt a jolt of pure joy. It was like I'd climbed a mountain and planted my flag.

Perseverance is one of those words that's all through the Bible. So is *patience*, with stories about sowing and reaping that don't mean much to a boy from Queens. But I learned about the deep-inside-your-own-self happiness that comes from sticking with something hard. Those long hours with the only thing Dad left us, that was what turned me into a musician. That's what made me stick with my songs when everything else in my life seemed to fall away.

I started seventh grade in West Islip with every intention of dropping out of school the second it was legal. I couldn't wait to hit sixteen so I could hit the road with a band, free and easy, sleeping as late as I wanted, playing music long into the night, a girl in every town and a heartbreak in every song. I heard the story of my own short life in the lyrics on Dad's old records. *"Losing you's a different kind of sad."* Those artists knew how I felt. *"I can hardly stand the pain of missing you today."* I couldn't wait to lay down my own pain, to hear my own self on the radio—to have the same connection with other kids sitting alone in their bedrooms with a record player as their best friend. *"I miss the gloom of the prairie moon that seemed to know my name."* Buck, Merle, and Johnny didn't have silky voices, didn't always hit the perfect note or have the best musicality or timing, but they had the things you can't put to words—the things you gotta feel to understand. Those boys drew you in because you knew that they meant every word of it.

Me and Mom and Dave had gone in thirds to buy our old Zenith record player. It was only sixty dollars, but that was everything I'd saved from my paperboy days. I protected that player like an heirloom, cleaning it every day, blowing off any dust that settled on it from Mom's woodwork, which she continued in our new house, and being careful to pick the lint off the needle. When any more money made it my way, I bought records of my own, starting with the Beatles and expanding into the Yardbirds, Bob Dylan, the Rolling Stones, and some more psychedelic stuff as I entered my teenage years. I'd find the chords and play with the band, standing in front of a mirror to see how I looked. My hair was black and thick, and I parted it in the middle and tied a bandana around my neck like some of the English singers. Someday, they'd scream for me like they did for John Lennon and the boys. I felt that in my bones.

When I couldn't afford records myself, I'd go to neighbors and friends and listen to whatever they had, which is how I got introduced to the blues. Son House, Mozelle Alderson, Memphis Slim, Pinetop Perkins, Lightnin' Hopkins: those fellas made you hurt with 'em. That was the same music Cash and Haggard were singing, only presented different. The beat felt like a slow march, like men hoeing a field. I got the sense that the cotton fields of the South were where this music started, which made me love the blues even more. I felt 'em. Those old-timey pickers made their way into all the songs I wrote later. I never met a one of 'em, but I knew their hearts. Blues pickers could bend notes like I'd never heard. I worked till my fingers cracked and bled to do what they did. I slid into notes with my old acoustic as best I could and tried to make my voice raspy and sore: "*Got up this mornin', feelin' sick and bad. / I's thinkin' bout the good time, that I once have had.*"

Practice wasn't work, even after the muscles in my hands and forearms started seizing up and the strings dug through the callouses in my fingers. I'd play till my back hurt so bad I had to lay flat on the floor, and then I'd play more down there. A lot of it was the burn to get good at music, to write songs and be in my own band. But music was also a cave for me. It was my armor, a place where I could retreat from everything else going on around me. Music was my own world. I did whatever it took to stay there.

Mom and Brian had two more boys, Brian Jr. and Bobby. I loved both of 'em, but I was real close to Bobby, the baby. He seemed so happy. I guess I wanted a little of that to rub off—to feel that joy that every boy loses as he gets a few years on him. I'd play music for Bobby when he was a baby. Once he got a little older, he'd clap and laugh whenever I broke out the guitar. Sometimes he'd slap the floor or the side of his bed to keep time, but he'd always be a half-beat off. I'd laugh, and he'd laugh louder. Those were some happy times.

"Promise me you'll stay in school," Mom said one afternoon, after knocking gently on my door and interrupting a jam session I was having with Brian Jones and Keith Richards of the Rolling Stones.

I stopped the record and said, "What?"

"I want you to promise me that you won't drop out of school—that you'll graduate," she said. "Get your diploma, then you can go off, do what you want to do. But you need to finish school."

It was like she'd read my mind, like she could tell I was counting the days until I turned sixteen. Dropping out and hitting the road with a duffel bag and a guitar, that's how I saw myself. Mom wanted to delay that life at least long enough for me to learn a trade.

"I will," I told her. "I'll get my diploma."

Keeping that promise didn't turn me into a model student. I hated almost every minute of school. The only exception was shop class, something that's all but vanished for kids today. My woodshop teacher took an interest in me and challenged me to take on tough projects. At the time, I had no idea what that meant. I'd made birdhouses in my grandpa's basement since I was a young kid. That wasn't much of a challenge. Maybe I should build a table, or a chair.

"I want you to make me a grandfather clock," Mom said to me one morning before I left for school.

She might as well have asked me to build one of the Apollo spaceships.

"Mom, I don't know how to do that," I said.

"It needs to be seven feet tall," she said, as if she hadn't heard me. "And I want it to have one of those pendulum arms that swings back and forth."

I went to school with a knot in my gut wondering how I was gonna build something that big and complicated. When I told my shop teacher, his eyes narrowed and he stared at me for a couple of seconds, like he was sizing me up.

"Go the library," he said. "Find some plans. Study 'em, then bring 'em to me when you think you're ready to start."

I jumped right in, digging through woodworking books and craft magazines until I found plans for a grandfather clock with a pendulum, just like Mom wanted. I studied those plans, sometimes closing my eyes and walking through the process in my mind, cutting, and planing the wood, notching it just right,

---

working the sander. When I thought I was ready, I took the plans to my teacher. He wasn't the smiling type, but I noticed that his cheeks weren't hanging in their normal frown.

"Get to work," he said.

It must have taken two months, maybe longer, an eternity for a kid who can barely see beyond the next Friday. I spent time making it as perfect as I could, realizing that I'd never get it exactly the way I wanted. Some things are never finished; they're just abandoned. I sanded it and got it as smooth as I could before I added a chestnut stain. When that dried, I sprayed sealant, slow and steady, keeping it even. No dust could settle in before it dried. I studied every inch to make sure. Then I added the guts of the clock, and then the face. Finally, I stood it upright and attached the pendulum. I held my breath before starting it. I'd put the level on it a hundred times, but I still fretted. It had to be balanced or it wouldn't keep time. Five, ten, fifteen minutes passed with the arm rocking back and forth, almost hypnotizing.

"I think you got it," my teacher said.

That was the first time since my dad walked out that I remember standing taller, feeling lighter and stronger—not higher than anybody, but sure not lower. I wanted people to know my name and to see what I'd done. Where there had once been nothing but a pile of wood, I had built a thing of beauty, something that would last. Something important. I didn't want that moment to end.

Thank the Lord I didn't have that clock with me in Nashville. I'd like to believe that maybe I wouldn't have sold it for drugs. But deep down, I don't.

———

At fifteen, I joined my first band with an older kid named Ron Daisley, a rebel who was always getting kicked out of school for some infraction or another. We played rock covers in front of whoever would listen—family, mostly, but we'd occasionally get a crowd near school or in a parking lot as folks headed to the beach for the Fourth of July. We weren't very good, but we didn't lack for confidence. I gave as much as I had in those early gigs. The work I put into that band was like the work I'd done on the clock: long and detailed. I'd get tight about it, worrying about how we sounded and if we'd practiced hard enough to make a song sound right.

Dedication and detail don't always bring you closer to God, but doing good work sure does lift your spirit.

We never got paid, which meant I had to find a real job. When I turned sixteen, one of my bandmates, another older kid named Freddy Avenaw, got hired to bag groceries at Waldbaum's. I wasn't experienced enough to be a bagger, but I could haul carts back in from the parking lot, which is what I did for a dollar and forty cents an hour. That first week, the second we got a little money, Freddie and me talked an older guy into buying us each a sixteen-ounce Falstaff beer. I chugged it in about three gulps.

From that moment forward, I was an alcoholic.

You don't know the moments in your life that change you until they've passed. I didn't think about that Friday afternoon again for a lot of years. Looking back, that was the fork in my road, the point where I took a wrong turn. Of course, I'd heard all the moral lessons about avoiding drunkenness. But that was for other folks. Not me. I could handle it. I was a kid doing what kids do, or so I thought. I didn't realize I was different. Alcohol had been a part of our lives forever, but we never thought much of it. Grandpa always had a few pops at the beach, or up at Uncle Ben's before driving us home. We'd laugh at him for slowing down every time he met an oncoming car, because he was drunk. Of course, my original dad had liquor on almost every breath he drew, and Dave drank as much as any teenager, probably more.

I was slow to develop, but once I had that first taste, I made up for lost time. After every paycheck, and sometimes in between, Freddie and me would play a couple of Rolling Stones tunes while we downed a six-pack each of longnecks. Then it was off to whatever bar we could fake our way into. Nobody really checked IDs back then. This was the sixties. Kids were getting drafted to go fight in Vietnam. Nobody cared if a couple of sixteen-year-olds had a few beers at a neighborhood pub. Besides, my hair was so long by then that the faculty at my school refused to let my picture appear in the yearbook. If I let that hair hide my baby face while standing in the middle of a crowd, nobody'd question my age.

From the get-go, I craved the drink. I didn't do it to be cool or to take an edge off; I didn't drink to make it easier to talk to girls the way some of the guys did. I drank because I loved it— because I needed it. Once I started, I didn't stop until the last drop vanished. Drinking wasn't something you did to be social, or so I figured. It was something you attacked—something you put the hammer down and went after full throttle. Every hour I worked, every dollar I made, was so I could drink. I thought about it in the morning and in the evening. Besides music, partying with a bottle and some buddies was all there was in the world. I was like a dog in front of a bag of food. I'd drink till I was sick. Then I'd purge and start again.

Things I worried about before started to fall to the back of the line. Music was still important, but I didn't practice the same hours I did before. I didn't fret about the songs the way I had. I sure didn't worry about my looks as much. If a night came down to working through one more set, getting one more gig, or going to a wide-open party, I was cracking open a bottle and ripping it up the road.

Sixteen slipped to seventeen, junior to senior year, and drinking made the jump to drugs without so much as a hiccup. I never cared for the taste of marijuana, so I went straight to LSD. John Lennon dropped acid. I wanted to be like him in every way. He had an Asian wife he got high with, so I got an Asian girlfriend and talked her into dropping acid and letting me photograph us nude, just like John and Yoko. You couldn't go after LSD quite like alcohol. I learned to pace myself. I also learned that tequila slows a trip and keeps it from getting away from you. I learned that a good trip seemed to make everything better. Jokes were funnier, music was finer, girls were sexier, and I was greater at everything I did. But a bad trip could send you over a ledge—paranoid and terrified of everything that moved, and a lot of things that didn't. Acid was like a big, stray dog. It could be gentle and fun, or it could bite you.

———

I also learned that the market for LSD was bigger and wider than I'd imagined. Men in suits bought tabs on their way to the train station. It wasn't legal, but it wasn't considered a ghetto drug. "Mind expanding," I heard a lot.

A poor kid—a kid who can't ask a girl out for a hamburger, can't buy a cool jacket or a pair of jeans that aren't hand-me-downs from his brother—when that kid sees a way to earn fast money, you can bet he'll take it. Then and now.

I began dealing acid during my senior year of high school. In no time, I'd made enough money to buy a Gibson SG and a Marshall amp. Jerry Garcia used the SG. So did Robby Krieger with the Doors. Those boys were redefining music right in front of us. I needed what they had. A kid named Ronnie Benson, who played drums in my original band, dated a girl in Brentwood, a town or two over from East Islip. Through her, Ronnie met a couple of guys named John Tajenski and John Hall, who were gigging at bars. Because I had a Gibson and an amp, and I wasn't afraid to get out front and sing, the four of us formed a band we called the Purple Grass. We had a Hammond organ and a Leslie cabinet. With a little rehearsing, we could cover some psychedelic rock songs and throw in a couple of hillbilly-rock originals. We weren't real professional, but we were trying.

The downside was coming home. Mom asked me straight up, "Where'd you get that Gibson?" She knew guitars.

I felt like I'd been hit with a hot wire. "I got it from a friend," I lied.

She didn't say anything, but I felt a distance between us after that, one I wished I could make up. As commandments go,

"Honor thy mother" was one I'd kept pretty well, up till then. That lie hurt me. But I hardened up. After that, false witness became a lot easier.

———

I put on the cap and gown and graduated high school, just as I'd promised. Days later, I beat a path to Manhattan with a guitar and some high dreams. I taped tabs of acid inside my acoustic and sold enough to stay fed and high. I sure kept my supplier happy. You'd be surprised how easy it was. I'd just walk up to people on the street—businessmen, artists, merchants, whoever—and say, "Acid?" They'd either ignore me or say, "How much can I get for fifty bucks?"

Meeting people had never been a problem for me, so it wasn't hard to find places to crash. There were plenty of empty buildings, and if I played a song or two, people always stopped. One of them usually had a pad nearby. Begging a night or two in a strange apartment became common. I was, in effect, living the homeless life before the ink on my diploma dried.

It was exciting. We'd drop acid and go to a cheap theater in the East Village to watch *Magical Mystery Tour*, the Beatles movie that made no sense unless you were high. What money I had, I kept wadded in my pockets like gum wrappers. Being careful with cash never occurred to me because I'd never had much of it. The only bills I had were from my supplier and whoever happened to be feeding me that day. Sleeping on shag carpet felt good after growing up on hardwoods. Plus, a rug didn't spin like a bed when you'd overcooked things with the booze.

Speed was the next trip, mostly to pick things up when the booze slowed me down. A good upper could keep the night rocking no matter what else I'd ingested. I had a good chemistry lab going on inside—speed in the morning, acid in the day, and booze at night. 'Course, I wasn't against trying whatever somebody threw my way. Quaaludes made it into the mix, along with a rainbow of pills: Big Reds, Black Widows, Blues . . . I never knew what most of 'em were or what they did, but I took 'em anyway. It was the summer of Woodstock (I didn't go), and drugs were part of everyday life. Many folks figured out that this was bad, and they stopped altering their minds before things got out of hand. Others, me included, fell deep into addiction. Some people—too many—never made it out.

Plenty of positives came out of that summer of 1969. Not long after I got to Greenwich Village, I heard a record titled *The Gilded Palace of Sin* by a new band called the Flying Burrito Brothers. A couple of former members of the Byrds, Gram Parsons and Chris Hillman, had blended the best elements of country, folk, psychedelic, and rock into eleven songs that hit me like a hammer. That was the kind of music I needed to write and play, the kind I'd nibbled around the edges trying to find without much success. I started taking the elements of the hardcore country from my youth, the edge of Cash, the grit of Haggard, along with some of the bluegrass elements my mom loved, and incorporating them with the rock licks and rhythms I'd learned with the Purple Grass. Just like that, I not only discovered the kind of music that I wanted to play for the rest of my life, I started crafting my own sound—my own identity as an artist.

People noticed. I started getting some gigs in the city, although there were so many musicians playing on the streets and in open-mic nights at clubs everywhere in New York that it was tough for anything with a country bent to break out. One twang and folks in the city would write you off as a hick. I did play a couple of gigs alongside David Peel and his band, the Lower East Side. I didn't know him at the time and didn't think he was much of a musician. To my shock, Peel had a record deal and a good following of fans. He would later be mentored by my hero, John Lennon, who'd produce a record called *The Pope Smokes Dope* for Peel, which was banned in most of Europe.

Looking back, my problems at the time were venue and focus. The Village accepted all kinds, but my brand of music, which later would be called "alternative country," was about thirty years and thirteen hundred miles out of place. In hindsight, that was probably a good thing. Given how immature and high I was almost all the time, becoming a success at that point would have made me like a dog chasing a car. I wouldn't have known what to do if I'd caught it.

Record producers didn't get me, but musicians seemed to understand. I had a small but loyal crop of fans. Work didn't pay well, but it wasn't hard to find. I never made enough to get off the street or out of my regular rotation of crash pads, but I did have walking-around money, enough to go see Johnny Winter at the Fillmore East and catch Led Zeppelin's first New

York show. I was high for both of those and don't remember much. That turned out to be a common theme in my life for many years.

I never got arrested for dealing or for using in public, which, looking back, was nothing short of a water-to-wine miracle. My first arrest was actually for something I didn't do.

Me and a buddy, Andy, and a girl we were both with at the time—sin was easy and cheap, and I was in as deep as you could get—we all wanted to head up to Middlefield, Connecticut, to the Powder Ridge Rock Festival, which was about two and a half hours away. It was supposed to be Woodstock with better drugs. War, Fleetwood Mac, Sly and the Family Stone, the Allmans, Chuck Berry, Janis Joplin, Grand Funk, Van Morrison, Ten Years After—three days of the best acts of that time. 'Course, we didn't have any way to get there. I suggested we light out on foot and throw our thumbs in the air. Hitchhiking was common back then. Somebody was bound to pick us up and get us close.

We got lucky, or so I thought. This guy in Manhattan couldn't get his pickup truck started. He called Andy and me over and said, "If you can get this thing running, I'll take you all the way." Dave didn't teach me much about fixing cars, but I'd learned the basics just being around him. It took me and Andy about three minutes to get that truck cranked.

The four of us piled in the bench seat and partied the whole way up. Almost at the festival, we pulled over for a nature call. Parked on the side of the road, my zipper down, my head full of dope and tequila, that's when the cops rolled up. Everybody flew except me. I had about thirty dollars' worth of cocaine wrapped in tin foil in my pocket. Rather than run, I dug that stuff out and ate it before I was shoved up against the truck with my arms pinned.

The cops caught Andy and the girl, but our driver got away. That turned out to be a big problem. As I was in a holding cell, just about the time the coke kicked in, the cops started yelling, "Somebody better confess or you're all spending a long time in jail."

Confess to what? Jail? For peeing on the side of the road? It took some time, but through the fog of the drugs, I finally realized that the truck didn't belong to the driver. We'd been conned into helping him steal it. Once that sank in, I realized that I might indeed be headed to prison for a good, long stretch. Not only had I helped a guy steal a truck—got it running, in fact—we'd crossed state lines, which made it grand theft auto.

That was scary. Hearing those bars clang shut will jar you, especially when you don't know if you're gonna be put away for a long stretch. It should have been a wake-up call. That first arrest should have been the torch in my soul that I'd write about later. It should have jolted me off that rough road I seemed determined to walk. But it didn't. I realize now that when you're already a prisoner on the inside, jail doesn't rob you of much more than you've already lost.

I wish I could have seen that at the time. Maybe if the cops hadn't figured out what happened, maybe if they'd kept us locked up a little longer, I would have seen the light a lot sooner. But that wasn't God's plan.

All I lost that weekend was my guitar. Cops kept it. I guess they knew I wouldn't make a fuss.

At least the festival got canceled. They had a bunch of upset people sitting at an empty ski resort dropping acid for three days and clogging up the hospital. I guess it could have been worse.

———

My drifting days stopped for a time after an event back on Long Island when I was visiting my brother. Mom and Brian weren't real keen on my dropping in, especially given how I looked and what I'd been doing, so I went to Dave's body shop. He was doing all right working on cars, so I slept on the shop floor for a few nights. One afternoon after finishing a job, Dave said, "Let's go to the beach."

I told him I'd love to, but we didn't have a way to get there. This wasn't long after my afternoon in jail for the stolen truck mix-up. That memory was too raw for me to take up with strangers.

"Sure we do," Dave said. He pointed to a Lincoln in the shop, one that was due back to the customer in a couple of days.

A voice in my head screamed that this was a terrible idea, but Dave was my older brother. Cutting loose with him was worth a little risk. So off we went, sharing a bottle of vodka as Dave ripped that car down to Cedar Beach where we'd played as kids. We got there as the sun was setting, low and large. The tide had rolled out. It was beautiful.

A lifeguard beat a path toward us as we stumbled onto the

———

sand, drunker than we should have been, but not as high as either of us had been that week.

"Beach is closed!" the guard yelled to us.

We pretended we didn't hear him, which caused the guard to pick up his pace.

"Hey, the beach is closed," he said again.

"Then leave," Dave said. "We'll be good."

"No, you have to go."

More words were exchanged until a fist flew, wild and round, nowhere close to contact. Dave didn't take to slights, and he'd fight anybody he thought had insulted him. The problem was, he wasn't that good at it—especially drunk.

The lifeguard retreated. "I'm calling the cops!" he yelled, pointing at Dave.

"Dave, we gotta go," I said.

I didn't have to tell him twice. We beat it out of there in the "borrowed" Lincoln, but not before the cops, who must have been close, found us. Now we had us a high-speed chase along the narrow streets of Long Island. Dave took a corner too fast and sideswiped a guardrail. I could hear the bumper and quarter-panel crunch and grind. But we kept going.

At one point, I closed my eyes and buried my head in my lap, so I have no idea how Dave got away from the cops. He made three or four more turns and took us back to the shop through a back entrance.

"What are we gonna do about the car?" I asked, convinced we were going to jail, if not for running from the law, then for wrecking a stolen car.

"Don't worry about it," Dave said. Then he called a buddy and said, "Johnny, I need you to steal a car."

A few hours later, a couple of hard-looking guys delivered a Lincoln to Dave's shop: the same make, model, and color as the one we'd crashed. Dave chopped the stolen car, replaced the wrecked parts, and returned the Lincoln we'd crashed to its owner, who was thrilled by the quality of the work.

That night I decided I had to get off the street and get a day job while I worked on my music. We could have been locked away for years, maybe decades. And for what? A couple of minutes of sunlight at a beach we'd seen a hundred times?

I hitchhiked my way up to Hauppauge and stayed a few nights with a musician buddy from my Purple Grass days named George Hoffman. He and another buddy of mine decided we'd all move into this house and share rent and expenses while we played music.

Within a couple of weeks, I had a job in a woodworking shop making custom doors and cabinets. I loved it. Something about the creation of a beautiful, sturdy piece—a thing that could be used and admired by a family for years—made me happy. Plus, the woodwork rounded me out in some ways. Wood lasted. You could look at it, touch it, knock on it, pass it down to your kids. Plus, it wasn't subject to somebody's opinion. A door either fit or it didn't. When a song ended, nothing remained but feelings and memories, good or bad. I needed both sides of that coin: the part you could see, and the part you could only feel. Music and woodwork did it.

One day on my way home from work, I stopped in for a

beer at this random roadside place, the sort of joint I assumed Johnny Rivers and the Rest Tones played back in the day. When I went in, the music hit me in the same way the Flying Burrito Brothers had the first time I heard them. The band was called New Hope, a hard-edged country band with a guy named Don Rasmussen playing the pedal steel and guitar. That music touched my spirit, so in the break, I went up to Don and said, "I can't believe you're playing this stuff on Long Island. This is what I grew up hearing."

Don and me became fast friends and bandmates. We formed a group called Duke the Drifter and the Angels in Overdrive. I was Duke. It was a play on Luke the Drifter, which was the name Hank Williams went by in the early 1950s when he was recording Christian music, a fair amount of which was spoken word. Me and Don wrote and played the kinds of songs we loved, a mixture of Gram Parsons, Greg Allman, and what I think Hank Williams would have sounded like with a Gibson SG, an amp, and some electric backup.

We played a lot of clubs on Long Island, sometimes venturing down into New Jersey and a few spots up near Westchester and Rye. Any place that would pay to have us, we'd play. Some folks liked it and others thought we were out of place. Most enjoyed hearing something different, a kind of music that, if you grew up in New York, you might never have heard in your life.

One of the places we played was a bar in Setauket called Chester's. That's where I met and became friends with Buddy Miller, who would come in and play with a band called

St. Elmo's Fire. This was thirty years before Buddy had the Album of the Year and a good ten before he put the Buddy Miller Band together with Shawn Colvin. I just knew him as a good musician who loved old-style country. We hit it off and would jam whenever Buddy was on Long Island. He'd have me up onstage to play a song or two with him during his set, and I'd do likewise when the Angels in Overdrive played. Sometimes we talked about hitting the road together, but I never thought anything would come of it.

Life was good. I built doors and cabinets in the day and played the music I loved at night. In between, I wrote songs and did enough drugs to kill a zoo full of elephants.

One night my drummer, Richard, and I were hanging out in the house waiting on a shipment of heroin to be delivered. By that point, there wasn't a drug of any kind that I hadn't tried. Rock cocaine, meth, synthetics, opiates—I'd done it all and enjoyed most of it. Later, a psychologist would tell me that my personality was a combination of impulsive, addictive, and self-destructive. That was like telling me water was wet. I knew what I was. At that time, I liked it.

When the heroin arrived, three guys from the mob walked into our living room wearing black trench coats and trying to give us tough-guy stares. Me and Richard weren't into power plays. We just wanted the drugs. Then a girl walked in behind them, a rail-thin beauty who looked just like Joni Mitchell.

For a second, I couldn't speak. For all my bad-boy behavior, I was never that great at the sex part of "sex, drugs, and rock and roll." I always saw women as God's precious gift, and even when I did a lot of things that I knew displeased him, I tried to be respectful to women. It didn't always work out, but it wasn't for lack of trying.

This girl made my heart race. She and her escorts dropped off the heroin and Richard paid them. I couldn't let her leave without saying something. So I blurted out, "Don't I know you from somewhere?"

She laughed and said, "That's the worst line I've ever heard."

It was, and I didn't say anything else until they were about to leave, when I said, "Hey, I gotta know your name."

She smiled, looked over her shoulder, and said, "Lynn." And they were gone.

Then I grabbed Richard and said, "You gotta get that girl's number."

A few days later, he came through, telling me her last name was Lovelace. I called and reminded her that I was the guy with the world's worst line. She remembered and accepted an invitation to come back out to the house.

"Richard, I gotta borrow your room," I said. "Mine's a wreck. It'd take a week to clean it, and I still wouldn't take a date in there."

When Lynn came over, she went through Richard's record collection and said, "Wow, I wouldn't have thought you'd like these guys."

I said, "Oh, yeah, I love them," having no idea what Richard listened to.

Lynn made an impression that lasted a lot longer than the drugs she delivered. I thought about her a lot, hoping to see her in the audience at one of the clubs we played. That didn't happen, although I did take her out a few more times.

Then one night in November, with the coming of winter biting me, I got a call. "Duke, it's Buddy," Buddy Miller said. "You want to come to Austin, be in a band with me?"

We'd always talked about it, and now it was in front of me. I looked around. New York, New Jersey, Connecticut—that was all I'd ever known. Austin, Texas, was the country-and-western capital of the world. If any place would understand my music, that would be it.

So I did it. I quit my woodworking job and told my bandmates good-bye. Then I loaded up a duffel bag, walked out to the expressway, and stuck my thumb in the air, just me and a German shepherd named Harold that had wandered up to the house and I'd started feeding. The two of us, me and the dog, hitched from Long Island to the Texas Hill Country.

Just like that, I was homeless again.

CHAPTER 4

PIECE OF HEAVEN HEADED STRAIGHT TO HELL

My first song was a country ballad called "Bottom of My List." I wrote it when I was about sixteen, and it sounds like it. 'Course, I thought it was the greatest piece of art ever created, until I wrote my next song, and the one after that. After a while you look back on your early stuff and realize how much you didn't know.

As I creep closer to seventy years old, I've finally learned that the same thing happens in your faith. You might meet the Lord early, in my case through my grandparents' church in Babylon, New York, in the fifties, but at that point you're like a kid picking through his first song. As good as you think you are, you aren't mature enough to polish the melody up—not experienced enough to spend extra time finding the right lyric. You grow in faith by reading the Bible, praying, trusting, reflecting every morning on what kind of person you were yesterday and what kind you hope to be today. Without all that, you're stuck on the first verse of a song you'll never finish. Nobody's born a natural musician. You might take to it better than most, but if you don't focus, practice, worry, and want it more than food, nobody other than family and close friends is gonna listen to you. Same with God. If you don't hunger and thirst for right-eousness, working at it every day, you're still a believer, just not one with a lot to say.

It took half a century for that lesson to take hold. I hope you'll learn from my path and take a different one.

Buddy Miller was one of those people who'd rather play music than eat. You could see the drive in him. If a wall stood between him and making it in the business, he was going around it if he could, over it if he couldn't, and through it if he had to. I saw that back in the early days when he was playing Long Island bars. Even then he was being called a country version of Eric Clapton, patient and confident enough in his licks to cre-ate something you remembered. Buddy didn't have any trouble finding paying gigs. He'd been the lead guitarist and backup vocalist for Johnny Cash, Linda Ronstadt, and Levon Helm. In the years after we played together, he made music with Shawn Colvin, Elvis Costello, Emmylou Harris, Steve Earl, Patty Griffin, Robert Plant, and, of course, with his wife, Julie Miller, all while traveling and recording with his own band.

———

No matter how many honky-tonks, biker bars, and cornbread festivals he played, Buddy always saw past the sawdust floors and beer bottles. He never seemed to mind the all-night car rides. The prize was always in his sights. It was like Buddy could already hear his name being called for Album of the Year, already see himself as the Country Music Hall of Fame Artist-in-Residence forty years before it happened. The gigs we played were just process.

I didn't think like that. I wanted to make records and be a star, but my notions of how to get there were fuzzy. Me and Buddy met through a girl named Gail Allen, who played and sang in the Angels in Overdrive for a while. She took me to hear Buddy at a club in New Jersey and then brought him to hear us. He was a couple of years younger than me, but we had a lot in common. We weren't Southern boys—Buddy grew up in Ohio—and we'd played rock and roll as kids. We'd both seen Led Zeppelin at the Fillmore East in '69—Buddy was sixteen and I was eighteen—but rather than imitating Jimmy Page, we both drifted back to our roots and wrote songs like the ones we'd loved as kids. Buddy'd grown up listening to the Haight-Ashbury music of Moby Grape and another California band called Love. I had gone from Jefferson Airplane to the Flying Burrito Brothers. When we got together, our own sound landed somewhere between Bob Dylan and Cliff Carlisle.

Getting together wasn't that easy. The trip from Long Island to Texas took a good week, maybe a day or two longer. Harold helped. A long-haired hitchhiker with a guitar and a duffel bag could walk a good long stretch without catching a ride, but a man with a dog was always good company. We didn't get off Long Island before the first long-haul trucker gave me a lift to just outside Roanoke. A night in the George Washington National Forest and I caught another ride in a pickup truck through the mountains down to Kingsport, Tennessee. We stalled a little there, and I had to play on the street to make some money. Folks were happy to give a bite of their sandwiches to Harold, but they weren't as quick to give me a buck or two for a burger. I'd left New York with a wad of bills after cashing my last paycheck from the woodshop, but eighteen hundred miles on foot ain't cheap.

Me and Harold caught another truck in Johnson City that got us to Nashville, where we hung out for another bit. That was my first trip to Music City—my first trip anywhere, really—and the memory of what I saw there—the Ryman Auditorium, Broadway, Second and Fourth Avenues—those visions stuck with me for a lot of years.

There wasn't a lot between Nashville and Memphis in those days, so we had a lonely couple of stretches where I wondered if I'd done the right thing. Most folks don't know—I didn't at the time—but when you're in Bristol, Tennessee, you're closer to Canada than you are to Memphis, Tennessee. Maps sit flat, so you don't get a sense of how much the curve of the earth spreads things out east to west. Pine Bluff, Fordyce, Hope, Texarkana, Linden, Tyler. When you grow up and spend your life in New York, where everything you need is within a few blocks—no more than a mile or two away at most—venturing into the country jolts your system. I didn't think we'd ever get to Texas, and once we did, we still had nearly four hundred miles to go.

Churches were always a good stop. Folks there would feed you. I got the stink-eye from a couple of parishioners, but I knew enough gospel songs by heart that they figured out that I was harmless, probably a drugged-up hippie, but not one who'd cause any trouble. My Queens accent didn't play well once I hit Tennessee, Arkansas, and Texas. If I hadn't had a loyal German shepherd, some of the folks we ran across likely would have whipped me just for the practice. Even the friendlies down in Texas, and there were quite a few, weren't easy. That last four hundred miles was anything but light. One fella had us sit in the back of a two-ton flatbed where we rattled, for what seemed like half a day, past signs for places called Log Cabin and Gun Barrel City. More than a few times I thought about hopping off and throwing my thumb in the air the other direction, heading back to New York where at least I knew the terrain.

The Hill Country was beautiful until a thunderstorm rode up on us. Even Harold had had enough by that point. We jumped out and found some shelter at a Sinclair gas station. The next morning we rolled into Austin, dirty, tired, hungry, and half a fuse away from blowing up.

I offered to wash dishes at a diner near the interstate if they'd let me eat a couple of meals and clean up in their restroom. A woman who looked like she'd been around long enough to have fought the Comanche and tough enough to have won gave me some bacon and eggs and told me to leave the bathroom cleaner than I found it, which I did. Then I found a pay phone and started calling Buddy. He didn't answer the first couple of times, and I was beginning to worry that I might have to sleep on the street. Finally, I got through to him. He rode out and picked me and Harold up, and we crashed at his apartment for a couple of days.

Buddy set me up at a place in Austin with the drummer and the bass player, but we didn't spend much time there. When we weren't rehearsing, we were on the road. We hit every bar in Texas, riding hard in an Econoline van that couldn't outrun a fat man. It had no windows other than the ones on the driver's and passenger's doors and only one back seat. That thing rode like a freight train. My seat was on top of one of the speaker covers, which meant I slipped and slid every time we made a turn. Still, I didn't mind at first. Everything was new to me—cowboys, accents, trucks, guns. I'd seen New Yorkers dress the part, but once you spend time in Texas, you realize what the expression "all hat and no cattle" means. This was a vast country of hard, free people.

Texas is bigger than every nation in Europe. For scale, it would stretch from Hamburg, Germany, in the north to Rome, Italy, in the south, and west to east from Paris to Krakow. If you moved Texas east of the Mississippi so that Texarkana sat in Manhattan, El Paso would be in Saint Louis, and Brownsville would tickle the Georgia-Florida line. Sometimes it felt like we covered every square inch of it.

Writing got cleaner and better. Being around a musician like Buddy will make you focus on being creative. Looking back, I see that Buddy taught me a lot of lessons, but none worth more

----

than realizing that creativity is work. Like all work, you've gotta make the time to do it and take the time to do it right. Every day Buddy would write—sometimes a little, sometimes a lot, but the sun never set without him putting something down. A lot of times he'd sit in a hotel room early with a cup of coffee and wouldn't come out till he had a bar or two written, maybe a whole song. If we were on the road that time of day, he'd close himself off in an office, or a closet, or lock himself in the van, but he was gonna write. Putting himself away was a routine. That routine became a habit. And that habit eventually made Buddy one of the most creative geniuses in the business.

For months I loved the adventure of traveling the rolling hills from Utopia to San Antonio and the barren moonscape from Abilene to Amarillo. The music was great. Buddy could play lead, rhythm, bass, or mandolin while singing lead or backup, something I'd never seen before. He amazed all of us. It's hard to measure how much I learned musically during that time. I sure learned how to play a show exhausted, how to push through distractions so the music didn't suffer, how to leave everything onstage every night, and how to write in the dark at a smoky bar or in the back of a van.

Goodness, we jammed. My hair was black and thick and long, and when I loosened a couple of buttons on my shirt and tied a bandana around my neck, there weren't a lot of nights I didn't draw a healthy crowd of smiling honeys. Club owners loved us. If girls were happy, guys tripped over each other like rats in the dark trying to buy 'em drinks. And those kids loved what we played like nothing I'd ever seen. A honky-tonk set in a New York club might draw a handful of fans and a couple dozen curiosity seekers. In Texas, anything that didn't include steel guitars was sissified city pop, the kind of thing that'd get a man run out of town with buckshot in his bumper. So they'd hoot and holler for this song or that, and me and Buddy and the band would draw it out and give 'em everything they wanted. Those were some long, good nights.

The road wore thin quick, though. I've never been a fan of the music lifestyle. Even now, I don't enjoy being in a train or a car, and I hate flying. I don't like staying in hotels, no matter how nice they are, and I'm not a big fan of eating every meal in a restaurant. That's not a life; that's making a living. Throw in the fact that with Buddy I was making about twenty dollars a show and living on jerky, soup, vodka, and cocaine (and sometimes making due without the jerky and soup), and it was easy to see I wasn't gonna make it.

Buddy thrived out there. He fed off every mile. I couldn't do that—not then. Harold the dog died. I was lonely and couldn't get Lynn Lovelace off my mind while all the cowgirls and low-slung roadhouses in Texas started looking the same. I called Lynn a lot. Just hearing her outer-borough accent and news from New York made me feel better. My heart hurt when we'd hang up. I remember one night in Lubbock, putting the receiver of a pay phone back in its cradle and watching a storm roll in from a couple of hundred miles away, swarming the distant plains like a war party. I looked at those black clouds roiling and rumbling for a long time. When we got to Austin, after more shows in Fort Worth and Waco, I packed my duffel bag.

———

I never gave leaving a second thought—never thought the matter through much at all, really. I just got it in my head that I needed to be home, so I walked to the road and threw a thumb in the air. Lickety-split, like it didn't mean a thing.

I never told Buddy I was leaving and never said good-bye to a soul. I wasn't mad at anybody—I loved them. But I never could hold an impulse inside me for more than a second or two. If it popped into my mind, I did it.

There were always consequences when I did things like that—and I did stuff spur of the moment almost all my life, sometimes with terrible and long-lasting consequences. It's amazing how a decision, made in an instant, completely changes everything. It's also true that regret sneaks up and hits you in the mouth when you least expect it—not once or twice, but hundreds of times. I don't regret getting off the road with Buddy when I did. I wasn't ready for that life. But I've woke up many a night wishing I'd handled it better. You'll never be remembered for your possessions or how much money you made. But how you treat people might as well be tattooed on your face. I owed Buddy and my friends better than to sneak away like that. It was a lot of years before I got to tell him how sorry I was for doing it, but at least I eventually got that chance.

I took a lot of wrong turns in life, many of 'em in a split second, with no deeper thought than I'd give to eating a potato chip. I know God's plan put me where I am, but I still think about those poor choices. Thirtysomething years after I walked out of Texas, I was living under a bridge while Buddy Miller was producing a record and touring with Robert Plant and the Band of Joy. One February night they had a concert in Nashville at the War Memorial Auditorium, exactly one mile from where I was sleeping in the Nashville Rescue Mission. I thank the Lord I didn't know about it at the time. I don't think I could bear to have heard Buddy playing and singing those same songs me and him heard Plant and Led Zeppelin play live in '69.

———

Lynn had moved out to Long Island Sound onto a place called the Chandler Estate, which used to be a girls' summer camp in the beautiful woods behind the cemetery of the Congregational Church of Mount Sinai. The Chandler family bought the property sometime in the thirties and turned it into a waterfront resort on Mount Sinai Harbor. Marilyn Monroe had spent time in the cottages in the fifties, and the government of Switzerland had put up some of their diplomats there, although that'd caused some confusion when residents mistook the Swiss flag for a satanic banner.

By the time Lynn got there, Miss Chandler, a strong old woman with long white hair and bright blue eyes who'd out-work most men half her age, had converted the cabins into makeshift apartments and a kind of boardinghouse. The place had fallen on hard times, which was why Lynn, who'd never worked and lived off welfare, could afford to stay there on her subsidy check.

I lucked out on the way back north, catching one truck from Austin to Atlanta and another from Atlanta to I-95 outside of

Raleigh, North Carolina. From there it was a straight shot—three truckers, some bad coffee, and just enough sleep to keep me from losing my mind. When I blew in to the Chandler Estate, Miss Chandler was pouring gravel into a pothole in the driveway. I dropped my duffel bag and helped her. It felt good to see pea gravel and black dirt again. Texas had plenty of rocks, red and brown, and hard clay ground where oak trees grew about as high as a basketball hoop before the wind beat 'em down. Throwing a shovel into some rich Long Island soil was a sign that I was home.

When me and Miss Chandler smoothed out the gravel, she thanked me and asked me how long I planned to stay. "Depends on if you'll hire me as a handyman," I said. After a minute of talking about music and my adventures in Texas, she gave me a job cleaning up the grounds, repairing the cottages, and doing general odds and ends on the property. I could sleep in any cottage that wasn't occupied and visit Lynn every day.

Lynn had a two-year-old son named Harlan when I first met her. He lived with her sometimes, but spent most nights with his grandfather. Looking back, that wasn't a very stable environment for a young boy. Kids need a place and a routine. It doesn't have to be a palace. A hut will do. But it ain't good to shuffle 'em between family members like a casserole dish nobody wants. Harlan lit up when he came out to the Chandler Estate. He'd latch onto Lynn and squeeze her till his little arms shook. Now I see that was his way of saying that he needed her to be there every day.

I enjoyed spending time with Harlan, watching birds near

the church and chasing rabbits through the woods. I was still young and didn't understand or appreciate what kind of influence I was having on him. Men forget what boys need. If I'd been older, I would've done more to help shape Harlan. He wouldn't leave my side when we were together, even if I was doing something dirty and hard like digging a hole or pruning bushes. He'd stick right with me. Kids need attention, not because they're selfish, but because that's how they connect with the world; that's how they learn to work, act, and behave. I didn't have enough of that when I was Harlan's age. I wish I'd given more of it when I was a younger man. Leaning on my heavenly Father now, I realize how much we all need guidance and how much the laws of the Bible continue to shape the civilized world today.

Ol' Ramesses, the only Egyptian pharaoh mentioned by name in the Bible, had eight wives and a hundred and three children. Reckon they didn't get much one-on-one time with Dad. That wasn't the exception. Outside of Jews and Christians, multiple wives and all kinds of kids who were shuffled around here and there—that was normal. What we consider Western values or American values are no such thing: they're Christian values.

Me and Lynn weren't living a Christian way. In fact, we lived the same homeless lifestyle that I had in Texas and Manhattan, only at an estate where finding an empty room was no more trouble than looking at the key board and taking what was left. Trouble was, we were doing it with a little boy, at least part of the time.

After a while, we drifted away from Mount Sinai, but stayed

on Long Island. I continued to play music and work whatever woodworking jobs I could find. Me and Lynn fell into a routine as predictable as rain. We'd fight, then we'd make up, then we'd party—and by party I mean the wide-open, sex-drugs-and-rock-and-roll partying that'd make the residents of Gomorrah look up to God and say, "Hey, you seeing this?" After the parties ended, we'd fight again and make up. I'd get mad and walk away from her for some silly thing or another. I can't even remember why we fought now. Drama follows drugs. Always. I should have married her sooner and stayed married to her longer. But like most things in my life at that time, if society thought you should behave one way, I was going the opposite direction. We lived in a den of drinking and carousing.

At some point during that time, I got my first DWI, which landed me in jail for a couple of nights. I thought nothing about it even though there should have been alarms going off. You'd think itchy jumpsuits and clanging bars would wake you up to the fact that something wasn't right—that it'd change you, get you thinking about straightening up, putting away the things you know are bad in your life. You'd think that, if you weren't an addict. The alcoholic and drug abuser writes off jail as a part of life, something you can excuse away or blame on somebody else. I didn't do much blaming, but I excused it. You drank, you drove, you got caught, and you went to jail for a spell. That was that.

Then, in 1984, with me sanding cabinets by day and playing bars on the weekends, Lynn got pregnant. A girl. We named her Leone. Four years later, with nothing much changed in the way we lived, we had a boy named Jacob. That's when we both decided that we'd been on Long Island long enough. Lynn wanted to head upstate, get a place with enough land for the kids—a place with something like the Chandler Estate nearby. That was a nice dream, but places like Miss Chandler's were becoming a thing of the past. The estate never got back to what it had been, and the land became a park when the county bought it after a fire leveled most of the buildings.

I got a road map, saw the Finger Lakes, and put my finger at the base of the largest one. "That's the spot," I said. "Let's go there." That was Ithaca, New York, which is where I spent the next thirteen years.

It would be great to tell you they were blissful years, but that would be a lie. Things went well for a little while. Lynn's mom had a little money and helped us get a place with a big yard and a barn out back where I set up a woodshop. I got a car and a good job, even had some side work making wood signs for local companies. I also put together another band. Paying gigs were easy with Cornell University right nearby. College kids enjoyed my music, even though most of them had never heard the artists like Hank Williams who'd inspired it. Of course, me and Lynn still fought. Kids add stress to the strongest relationships. When you've been bickering from the get-go, adding a couple of little ones to the mix speeds up the hotheadedness. Many a night, I'd walk away to the barn and have a drink just to get away from the tension inside.

Harlan stayed in our lives some, but Leone and Jacob took most of our time. A four-year-old girl's a handful. Throw a baby boy in the mix, with the crying and the diapers and the waking up at all hours, and I wondered more than once what I'd gotten myself into.

Then, one night as I was driving home from work, I saw a tall black man hitchhiking. I knew what it was like to catch a ride, so I stopped and told him to hop in. We hit it off just right, so I invited him to the house. He said he was an evangelist. Folks around the area called him Brother Phillips. That seemed strange to me. Why was a local preacher hitchhiking only a couple of towns over from his congregation? Lynn didn't say nothing, but I could see from her eyes that she thought it wasn't quite right either. Brother Phillips obviously wasn't in a rush to get anywhere, since he spent a good long while at our place. The longer he stayed, the more he drew me in. After a while, I didn't want him to leave. He glowed with goodness, which was just the kind of thing our house needed. I invited him to come back, which he did several times.

About the third time he was at our house, he asked me why me and Lynn weren't married.

"Just never got around to it," I said for lack of a better answer.

"I know how that is," he said with a smile. "But, you know, you're sinning in the eyes of God." He went on to explain that marriage was more than a legal proceeding or something society expected of you. It was a holy union, blessed by the Almighty. Not only did it formalize us as family, it would bring both of us closer to God, which would make our lives better. "Everything good in society, everything good throughout history, has started

---

with the stable family," he said. "A man and woman brought together by God. Two become one. That couple goes forth and multiplies, and God's pleased. What you're doing mocks what's right and good. That disappoints God, because he knows how that story ends."

It was like my grandmother was speaking through this preacher. I not only agreed with what he said, I felt an urgency about it—a sense that I had to marry Lynn right away to make things right by God and for my kids.

Then, just as I felt the call back to the church, it almost got stamped out. We went to the minister of the local Methodist church and asked about setting a date to be married.

"You already have kids, don't you?" the minister asked.

"We do," I said. "Girl and a boy."

"You can't be married here," he said, and turned his back on us without so much as a "good luck."

That ran me hot. Here we were trying to make our way back to God, to correct our sins and do the right thing, and a man of the cloth shut us out. I know now that this same sort of thing has turned countless people away from the church. A pastor shuns 'em for past sins; a deacon judges 'em pretty hard; they get a bad reception when they try to set things right and get back in touch with faith. It's no wonder churches have been shrinking for years. I've learned lately that if the church didn't take sinners, there wouldn't be anybody there at all. Breaking God's laws doesn't disqualify you from Christianity. It makes you the person Christ wants most.

After our little run-in with the Methodist preacher, Lynn

was over the whole idea of getting married. I would have been too, if Brother Phillips hadn't come back to the house a few days later. He asked how we were doing on the marriage front, and I couldn't wait to tell him about the treatment we'd received. I wanted him to condemn that Methodist minister for turning us away, but he didn't. He smiled, nodded, and said, "Good. I was hoping you'd let me marry you in my church."

A month later, me and Lynn walked down the aisle of an all-black church in upstate New York in front of our kids, my brother Dave, and about fifty members of Brother Phillips's congregation who came out to make us feel at home. We were so poor that Lynn baked our wedding cake, and some of the congregation, people I didn't know, brought covered dishes so we could have a reception. It was a beautiful day all around.

The only downer was Lynn's mom, who wouldn't come. That hurt us. I think she anticipated the trouble that would come. Brother Phillips must have sensed that Lynn was upset about her mom. He said, "It's nice having these people come out to celebrate with you, but the only witness you needed was God. And he's well pleased."

I don't know what those angels looked like who delivered messages in the Bible. They must have been something, since everybody was "sore afraid." But one who walked the earth in the 1980s was six five with skin the color of coffee grounds and a smile that would light up a moonless night; a hitchhiker who didn't have any trouble getting around after that first night when I picked him up; a man who reminded me what it felt like to find the Lord's blessing, what it meant in your soul to right a wrong. Brother Phillips didn't glow or sprout wings. But he was an angel. He surely was.

———

I do so wish I'd gone back to him a year later, gone back to that church, listened to him preach. I do wish I'd squeezed my eyes closed as he prayed. I wish I'd asked God to come back in and take hold of me, to calm my soul. The kids continued to be trying on a young marriage. Being poor had never worried us. We'd always teetered on the tightrope of poverty. Like all relationships born of drugs and alcohol, simple talk about things like who would run to the market for milk and diapers jumped quick from calm to vicious. I could go from a standing start to nuclear war in a matter of seconds, and Lynn could press the buttons to get me there.

In my mind, I was functioning as well as anybody. The needles were gone, especially after the kids were born, and cocaine cost more than gold. Vodka and weed were always around, and a new breed of pill popped up every couple of months, but I got by the way most addicts do: keeping a job, a house, and a life. At least that's what I told myself.

My little brother, Bobby, came to visit one weekend, and just before sunset I took him out to the barn to show him some of the sign work I was doing. While there, I cracked open a couple of beers and fired up a joint. I still wasn't a big marijuana fan, but like every other drug, if it was around, I wouldn't let it go to waste. Just about the time a relaxing blue fog nestled

———

over me and Bobby, the barn door opened and Lynn stormed in with her jaw set.

"I've had it," she announced. "I'm sick of the drugs. It's either drugs or family. You decide. You can't have both." To prove that this wasn't a discussion, she turned and slammed the door on her way out.

Bobby stared at me a second and then looked at the floor. I felt my heart race and my face flush. Yelling was one thing, but embarrassing a man in front of his little brother was something else. At least that's how my dope-filled mind processed things at that moment.

"Well, I guess that's it," I said to Bobby.

The next morning I packed a few things and left my wife and children for good. Over a joint and some hurt feelings.

Not a day goes by that I don't wish I could take it back. One of the early verses King Solomon wrote in Ecclesiastes says, "Patience is better than pride. Do not be quickly provoked in your spirit, for anger resides in the lap of fools" (Ecclesiastes 7:8–9). I wish Mom or Grandma or Brother Phillips had been there to read that verse to me. I wish I'd been strong enough, disciplined enough, steeped enough in the Spirit to have known it. To have lived it.

I moved in with various friends until I could get another place in Ithaca, close enough to see the kids but not so close that I would run into Lynn. Why I couldn't humble myself, calm my restlessness, do the things necessary to put my family back together and turn all our lives around, is beyond my ability to explain. It'd be easy to blame it on Satan, or drugs, or some deep, unresolved psychological thing from my past. But I know in my heart it was nothing so complicated. I walked away because, at the time, it was easy. I'd felt like I'd been pushed into a bad choice, so I said, "I'll show you," and I left. It never occurred to me at the time that this might have been the same sort of fight my mom and dad had the night John Harvey walked out on the Seegers, leaving us nothing but a name and some dusty records.

About a year after I left, I called Lynn and asked to speak to the kids. There was a thick silence. Then she said, "They don't want to talk to you."

That knife dug deep and left a scar I feel to this day.

———

For a dozen years I tried to stay close to the kids, to build lasting friendships and find a love to fill the longing I felt deep down inside. Then Oxy and Ecstasy became popular, so I had to give them a whirl. Rock cocaine laced with PCP was cheap enough, and if you mixed it with a chilled shot of gin or vodka, you could float for a full day. We called meth "ice" in the late eighties and early nineties. Pink ice was the quickest trip. I never knew why it was pink. To sum it up, there were plenty of times when I was the kind of man you'd run away from without a second thought.

Losing a deep connection with the children ripped out what parts of my soul the drugs didn't kill. No matter how much a man intends to do what's right by his kids, when he isn't at home for the little things like doing laundry, hearing stories from school, watching television, helping with homework, teaching them how to scramble an egg or hammer a nail—when he ain't there to set an example in ways big and small—well, that man eventually becomes a visitor, a spectator, a guest, welcome or not. That tears your heart one tiny shred at a time. *Sorry, Dad, I can't see you this weekend. Hey, Dad, can we push our visit to another day? I've got a date. Yes, a boyfriend. No, I didn't make the team.*

As the kids got older, the answers got shorter.

How you doing?

Fine.

How's school?

Okay.

What do you want to do this weekend?

I don't care.

My second and third DWIs came close together. That prompted my first stint in mandatory rehab, an evening program where I watched bloody videos of car crashes and heard the cries of families as they learned that their loved ones had been killed by drunk drivers. Counselors would ask questions that I didn't understand, things like, "How does alcohol make you feel?"

Drunk.

"What do you believe other people think about you when you drink?"

I didn't think about other people and couldn't have cared less what they thought.

"What do you think about yourself when you're not drinking?"

———

I thought about music, woodwork, what I was going to have for dinner—the stuff that folks thought about in the day.

After a while, the whole setup seemed like a money grab to me. Nobody showed much interest in us getting better. That would've put a stop to the cash they siphoned out of my paycheck every week. Once it became obvious that I would be there as long as I kept paying, I walked away from rehab.

My fourth DWI was like a cocked gun: it wasn't a question of if it was going off; it was just a matter of when and how much damage it would do. That DWI landed me in front of an unforgiving judge who rightly pointed out that I didn't show much interest in rehabilitation. He put me under house arrest. I had an electronic monitor strapped to my ankle. If I went anywhere other than work and home, I was in violation of my sentence.

Of course, there wasn't any leeway for getting a bite to eat on the way home or grabbing a beer—just one—with a friend. The third time I violated, the judge threw me in the Ithaca jail for six months. That was a hard stretch. Visitors were in short supply. I lost all contact with the kids. I'd given Lynn the perfect excuse to keep 'em away from me. I had a lot of time to think about that, alone with nothing but a thin cot and a stainless steel toilet in my cell. That six months also gave me a lot of time to dream. Everything came back to music.

I was a good woodsman. If you wanted a table, or a fine door, or a bookcase, I'd do you as solid a job as anybody. You'd be proud to show what I'd built to your friends, and I'd be proud for having built it. But music lifted me in ways that nothing else could. I couldn't let my life slip by without trying one more time to make it as an artist.

That wasn't possible in New York, even though it was the only place I'd ever lived other than my year on the road in Texas. My only chance was Nashville, somewhere near Broadway where Hank, and Chet, and Johnny all left their marks.

I straightened up for quite a few years. Got a girlfriend named Mary who worked in data processing. She was funny and smart, and I loved being around her right up to her first drink. Then she turned mean as a copperhead. She never insulted me until she drank. That's when she'd rip into me. Whiskey don't make liars. It makes truthful fools. I was one. I knew. Mary didn't only think the stuff she did about me because she was high—that was just when she said it. It wasn't long before we went our separate ways.

I worked in the woodshops and kept my nose clean until Jacob was a teenager. That's when I decided that too much life was gone. I was almost fifty years old. A new century was just around the corner. Time was running out. This was my last chance to make it in music. My priority after a hard day with a saw and a sander was finding a comfortable chair rather than songwriting. It was now or never. If the dream had any chance, I had to go.

I met my son outside Lynn's place. We sat in the front seat of my 1980 Buick, a beater with a Bondo quarter panel and no reverse, which made for some interesting parking jobs. That's when I explained to him that as much as I loved him, I had to ask his permission to let me give music a shot one more time—this

---

time in Nashville. "If I don't go now, I might never know if I could'a made it," I said to him. "This might be my last chance."

"Of course you gotta go," Jacob said as if it was the most obvious thing in the world. "Of course."

I put my hand on Jacob's head and ran my fingers through the boy's thick hair. I didn't wipe the water from my cheeks. Just let it run onto my lips, salty and warm.

———

You can tell when a fella writes about hard pain without feeling any of it. He tries too hard. Says too much. He can't get to the core, because he don't know where it is. Once you've been in a cell knowing nobody's coming to see you, and there's nobody to call—once you fought with a wharf rat for sleeping space under a bridge—you don't have trouble writing after that.

I hear artists nowadays talk about finding inspiration, about going someplace or another to find their sweet spot. That's never been a problem for me. All I ever had was a guitar and a note-book. More times than not, I'd found the notebook in the trash. But there was always something to write about, some word or feeling somebody'd given me in passing—maybe a smile from a stranger or a sad look from a rich but desperate man. I had a way of spotting the lead walls around a heart, the hurt you can't talk about because of the shame, the cold water that washes the past away, the slow death the bottle brings on the soul. I write about that.

I also write about redemption. That part comes from God,

through Jesus, who forgave me for all the terrible things I've done and uses me to show others the joy he brings. Christ uses my fingers and voice, and I'm glad to let him. In "Angie's Song," one of the tracks on my first record, there's a verse that says, "Let me be the one with his eye on faith."

That's what I pray these days.

People ask me how you write a song. Does the music come first? The words? Do you get stuck on a chord or a lyric? I can't answer that, because, for me, it comes from where I've been. It comes from deep down—places I describe but can't explain.

When I was playing on the street not long ago, a man went by, dead-eyed and shuffling. I knew where he was headed. I knew what was on his mind. He couldn't think past the next drink, the next hit, the next taste. Nothing or nobody mattered more than the high. I knew that man, and I knew that place. I'd been there. I'd been him. Just like that, I hit a couple of blues chords and wrote the first verse to the song "Zombie."

That was God. He saved me from my own destructive self so my voice could bring love and hope to others.

I was doing a radio show not too long ago and Emmylou Harris called in. She said, "We all write about it, but Doug lived it. He's the real deal."

That's half right. I lived the hard things in my songs. I saw a lot more. But our God, who gives us hope and shows us love, is the real deal. I'm just the messenger, allowed to live another day so somebody else might turn their own life around.

CHAPTER 5

"SETTIN' THE WOODS ON FIRE"

Reverse is a handy gear. And not just for your car. At some point, everybody wishes they could back up, take a different turn, run that stretcha road one more time in a different way. If I could throw life in reverse, I wouldn't have walked out on Buddy Miller the way I did; wouldn't have walked out on Lynn and my kids like I did; wouldn't have downed that first beer like I did, dropped that first hit of acid like I did, or stuck that first needle in my arm. 'Course, none of that's possible. Reverse don't work in life. What's done is done forever.

What we can do is hit the brakes and turn around when we're on the wrong road. We can turn the wheel and nose ourselves in another direction, get out of those places that damage us. We can make a left out of those relationships that we know are wrong. We can make a quick, hard U-turn when that soft, quiet voice in us starts warning us of trouble ahead. The Bible says, "Wide is the gate and broad is the road that leads to destruction, and many enter through it. But small is the gate and narrow the road that leads to life, and only a few find it" (Matthew 7:13–14). I found it, but not before traveling that broad road of destruction for many a mile.

Driving down to Nashville from Ithaca, I had to be careful not to put myself in a bad spot at the rest stops and gas stations. I couldn't just pull in anywhere, hop out, grab a soda, and be on my way. I had to plan and sometimes drive around awhile so the car always faced out. If I ever had to back up, I was out of luck. Reverse was just like neutral, so if I got blocked in I had to get out and push. The trip was just over thirteen hours by car, west to the Alleghenies and then south to Columbus, Cincinnati, and Louisville, before hitting the home stretch. None of it was easy. The Buick got a knock in the engine at the Pennsylvania line, and Interstate 71 had construction delays every ten miles. I almost ran out of gas twice, but at least I wasn't hitchhiking like the first time I'd made my way through Nashville. Still, I was quite a sight, chugging along in a Buick that looked like it might not make it to the next exit ramp, with everything I owned in the bucket seat next to me.

I stayed in the cheapest motels I could find, and I slept in the car a night or two until I found a mission where I could crash for free. The car wasn't quite wide enough for me to stretch out, but it wasn't bad. A little money had to go a long way as I searched for a place and a job. Cheap fast food and free coffee at the Kroger grocery store became my diet.

A couple of weeks in, I found a small rental house in East Nashville, and I got a day job making custom mahogany doors—big, heavy ones with ornate carvings. Some had lead-glass inlays and others had special hardware. Each door was like a song, a work of art that all of us in the shop helped to craft. Being the new guy, I didn't say a lot in the beginning, but I felt a lot of pride when one of those doors went into a big house in Green Hills or Belle Meade.

My coworkers smiled when I told 'em that I'd moved to town to make it in music. That was like a blonde waitress in Hollywood saying she'd moved out west from Iowa to become a movie star. Just like every one of 'em, I thought I'd be different. I believed my music would knock people off their feet, because nobody was singing and playing the old-style stuff anymore. Country music at that time had become pop music with fiddles, which was not a bad thing. I liked it. Still do. Nothing makes me tear up quicker than a Martina McBride song. Her voice reminds me of Mom's: strong and beautiful. But my music took people back to the days when Uncle Dave Macon was tearing up the banjo and Roy Acuff's fiddle carved a notch in your soul. *"I went to the scene of destruction / And a picture was stamped on my heart."*

Songwriter nights were as common as happy hours in Nashville. From Sixteenth Street to Broadway, you couldn't go more than a hundred feet without finding a place to play. Some clubs had you put your name on a list and you got to play an original song or two. At other clubs you had to wait for weeks. As many spots as there were to play, there were a hundred times more artists looking for a shot at being discovered.

My first open-mic gig was at a small restaurant called the Commodore Grille in a Holiday Inn next to the Vanderbilt campus. They allowed seven or eight songwriters to play between 10:30 and 11:30 every night except Tuesdays. I figured that was as good a place as any to test my material. I'd entertain a few college kids, maybe a businessman or two, knock the rust off my Duke the Drifter stage persona, work on my timing, and gauge where I stood compared to the rest of the acts that showed up. How tough could it be? I was sure I had more experience than anybody else there.

I drove the Buick downtown after work, still careful not to put myself in a place where I needed to reverse. I also got a quick bite to eat before signing up. When I was younger, I always wanted people to think I was cool, so I'd worry about getting somewhere too early, seeming too anxious. I tried to give off an air of not caring too much. Staring fifty in the face throws that attitude out the window. I cared a lot and didn't mind who knew it.

Acts had to be in the restaurant before eight o'clock. No call-ins, and no exceptions. I got there at six. My name was third on the list. Two songs, and you were allowed one other person to accompany you. All I brought was my guitar and what I thought were my best songs, at least the best to perform live.

I was right about having the most experience. None of the other artists had been born when I got my first paying gig. But the more I listened to 'em, the more I wanted to sneak out the back door. The talent was off the charts. One after another, these good-looking men and women got on that little stage and tore through some of the most soulful songs I'd heard in ages. They were poised and polished, and, man, could they play. Guitar, piano, mandolin, fiddle—it was like attending a master class. My first thought was, *These kids sound like they've been cutting hit records for years.* The songs had depth, maturity, and hooks that kept you humming long after the last note evaporated into the night air. I felt outgunned. My voice had never been polished, but I'd never tried to be a crooner. My niche was roots music before the genre had a name. That night it didn't matter. I wasn't in those other cats' league.

The house I'd rented was only a couple of miles from that Holiday Inn, but it seemed like a long, lonely stretch as I drove back after my first night back onstage. Once I closed and locked my front door, the silence hit me like a board. No family, no friends, and if that night was any indication, no prospects of making it as a musician in this town. That was the first time the hard hand of hopelessness hit me in the gut. As I lay in bed, I felt like I had a bag of wet sand on my chest.

Work was quiet for the next week or so. My routine stayed normal, but the feelings weren't the same. Every night, I'd go home and be overcome with loneliness, a physical pain from lack of human contact. I missed everybody from my earlier life. What I didn't appreciate at the time was how much that loneliness was a separation from God as well as my friends. I know that "he heals the brokenhearted and binds up their wounds" and that he is "a father to the fatherless," but at the time, I didn't feel like the Lord lived in that empty house with me (Psalm 147:3; 68:5).

Mom passed away from an undiagnosed lung infection. That hit me harder than I could have imagined. Humans are the only animals that know they're gonna die. That shapes us. Always has. It's the reason Jesus' resurrection is the miracle that changed the world. A fella predicting his own execution and telling everybody that he'd come back from the dead, well, that'll get your attention. When he pulled it off, all that stuff he'd said before—grace as the salvation of the world, love your neighbors as he loves you—those teachings take on a new meaning. For the rest of us, death lingers like a neighbor you don't want to see. I knew Mom was in heaven, but the grief of her going, along with the sadness I felt more often than I should, left me in a spiral.

I went to other songwriters' nights. The Bluebird Cafe, now famous because of the TV show *Nashville*, was always known to folks in the industry as a place to find undiscovered talent. Monday nights from six till nine, the stage opens up. Garth Brooks caught a break there, and so did Kenny Chesney and Dierks Bentley. A lot of the top songwriters in town polish their work at the Bluebird. Getting on that stage isn't easy. You gotta call at exactly 11:00 on Monday morning. It's like trying to win a prize from a radio station: the first twenty-five artists to sign up make it. And the list fills up quick. It was difficult for me to walk away from a job in the woodshop at 11:00 a.m., especially if we had a big project, but my boss understood what a big deal it was to play the Bluebird, so he let me sit in the office and make calls. After a couple of tries, I finally got through in the nick of time. I was number twenty-two out of twenty-five.

Then I had to get off work a little early, because you had to be in the club at 5:15 p.m. They reserved two chairs for each performer. The other twenty-four songwriters brought some-body, either a backup player or a fan to support them. I came alone, although some of the folks from work showed up a little after 9:00 p.m. and stood in the back to cheer for me. Them being there meant more to me than they'll ever know. It surely did. You only played one song. I was happy to have a crowd in there to listen, although by the start of the second hour, I felt like I should walk out. As good as the artists had been at the Commodore Grille, the ones at the Bluebird were three or four times better. To say I was overmatched doesn't do it justice. Those guys were playing seven different chess games at once while I was throwing dice against a wall.

The applause I got that night felt good, but I knew how I stacked up. Nashville was Music City for a reason. You could skip a rock down almost any street in town and hit a talented artist. A lot of 'em would blow you away. I'd written songs since I was fifteen, but there was a big difference between getting a club gig in Ithaca and making it in the country music capital of the world. How those folks at the Bluebird open mic weren't cutting hit records was a mystery I would never understand. But the more pressing question was, if they couldn't make it, where'd that leave me?

That night at home was rough. I'd been fired up to play the Bluebird, and I'd given it my best shot. Poured it all out on that stage. That'll drain you on the best of days. It's not so much the playing; it's the emotions you go through, the nerves you battle, and all the work you do in your own mind. A guy playing a couple sets of music at a club won't be onstage more than an hour and a half, maybe two. That would seem part-time to anybody who hadn't done it. Folks who have will tell you that it's the most draining thing you'll do. I've hauled lumber in the sun for eight hours and I've played a packed club for two. I can tell you that the club gig wore me out a lot more than the lumberyard.

Nerves make some artists temperamental. Something won't be exactly the way they want it backstage and they'll throw a fit, yell, and carry on like a spoiled baby. I never did anything like that, but once a show was over, I felt like I was falling off a cliff. All the buildup, all the focus I put into my performance, all the emotion I poured out during a show was always followed by a terrible low spell. Sometimes it'd just be an hour or two. Other times it'd linger for a day. Add the fact that there was nobody waiting when I closed the door at home, and it's easy to see how a man could tumble into a dark spot. That night after the Bluebird wasn't the darkest, but it was dim.

I threw myself into woodwork. I changed jobs and moved to a cabinet shop run by a man named Jack Roscoe, another angel who did his best to show me the right path. Jack hired a lot of part-time workers with Down syndrome. Woodwork, at least the parts that weren't real dangerous, was perfect for them. I didn't know much about Down syndrome. I'd grown up in a time when everybody with a developmental disability got lumped into the "retarded" category. That wasn't derogatory. It was just how we identified everything from autism to trisomy disorders. I went to school with some challenged kids, but as a fifty-year-old man it was embarrassing how little I knew about their abilities or needs. After working with them, I was overwhelmed by how kind, generous, honest, and hardworking they all were. That cabinet shop showed me how God's grace shines through all people.

I wish I'd been closer to the Bible back then. I might've thought about that part where Paul said if we are tempted, God'll provide a way out so we can endure it (1 Corinthians 10:13). I could have stood to hear that a time or two in those years. Jack Roscoe was one of those ways out God had provided. He was one of many safety valves against temptation laid out for me. I just wasn't ready to use them.

'Course I found a way to get fired from Jack's shop. It was petty, just the kind of small slight that I tended to blow into something big. There was a kid I didn't care for working a few feet away who kept side projects under his bench. That irked me. I saw it as an insult and theft from the company. Woodwork is not lucrative. There's no room for slacking. I'd gone to Jack about it several times, but it seemed obvious that he wasn't going to do anything. So one day as we packed a truck for a job, which was hectic and time sensitive, the kid took a piece of cardboard off my bench to help separate the wood on the truck. I kept that cardboard there to protect whatever wood I was working on at the time. Him grabbing it set me afire.

It sounds crazy. A piece of cardboard. But that was the drop that burst the dam. In hindsight, if he'd said, "Doug, you mind if I take this cardboard for the truck?" I would have said, "Sure, I'll get another piece." Or if he'd said, "Sorry I took your cardboard. We were in a rush," I would have said, "No problem" and let it go. But we were beyond that.

I said, "What are you doing grabbing that off my bench?"

He responded with, "Get out of the way. We've got a truck to load."

I cursed at him. He cursed at me. And I hit him in the jaw with a roundhouse punch that put him down.

Jack escorted me off the premises.

Three weeks went by. I needed work. Finally I went back to Jack and pleaded for him to rehire me.

"Do you know why I let you go in the first place?" he asked.

"I assume because I knocked that guy out," I said.

"No," he answered. "It was because when I asked you if you'd ever do something like that again, you said, 'Absolutely.'"

It wasn't my place to be stubborn and self-righteous, but those were sins I didn't consider at the time. The fact that Jack rehired me was another miracle, one I didn't appreciate fully.

I've since learned about how the Bible says that anyone who loves God must also love their brother and sister. Well, I punched a brother in the mouth. And another brother hired me back when I didn't deserve it.

———

The music dream didn't die, but I didn't see much of a path forward either. I hit all the songwriter clubs: Cafe Coco, which was a college-age crowd. Some of 'em got my music but most of 'em talked through my set. There was the Crescent Cafe, which had songwriter sets three or four nights a week. I also hit the Listening Room Cafe, which had some of the best acoustics in town. I tried to showcase some of my soulful stuff there. Mizz Tee's Honkey-Tonk, which had a Tuesday-night songwriters' jam festival—a fun time to pick and sing with other artists, but not a place where a guy like me would get noticed. Some talented cats jammed at Douglas Corner and Edgehill Studios Cafe where, if you were lucky, you might find yourself playing for the hottest producer in town. I hit 'em all.

Compliments flowed, but no offers. I got to know some people, and through them auditioned for a couple of gigs: backup singer for a female artist on the rise, and an acoustic guitar and backup vocal spot for another artist most music fans would recognize. I came close a couple of times, but none of it panned out. You can tell when people are being polite without being genuine. That happened some, but not often. Most of the time, people loved what I did, but I wasn't right for that job or that producer at that time.

Loneliness deepened each time I got turned down. It's hard not to take rejection personal. In your mind, you know that you can't fit everywhere. Folks might love your voice, but you aren't right for what they're working on right now. It was like having hickory when you needed oak. I was the wrong wood for the job.

I'd never worried much about my age up until that point. I always figured I had more years ahead of me than behind.

When you're thirty, you double it and figure you'll live past sixty. When you're thirty-five, you know you've got a good shot at making it to seventy. But once you turn fifty, then fifty-one, and fifty-two, you realize that you probably won't get to a hundred and four. Plus, the kids who were too young and inexperienced to best you when you were forty eventually hit their thirties—and their peak. That reality ought not sneak up on you the way it does. But, sure enough, you wake up one morning and see it, bright and hot as the rising sun.

I didn't think about Abraham being a hundred when he fathered Isaac, or Moses being in his golden years when he led the Jews out of Egypt. I was not thinking about God's plan for Doug Seegers. I was worried about myownself. My clock ran a lot faster than God's.

The average age of a pop star is twenty-seven, and the average time the good ones are on the charts is eighteen months. Country music skews a little older, but the average age of a charting country artist is thirty-one. You'll get guys like Kenny Chesney or Blake Shelton or a crossover artist like Darius Rucker offsetting kids like Hunter Hayes to bump up that average age, but you never see a first-time artist in his fifties or sixties. The quality of the music's irrelevant. Marketing people won't stand for signing a senior citizen who's never cut a record. The demographics don't work. If I'd had enough faith, I would have prayed and pressed on. But I didn't. I let the Devil fill me with depression instead.

I thought I was longing for company, for human companionship, a tender touch or a friend to talk to at home. What

I needed was a closer relationship with God. The Bible says, "Walk by the Spirit, and you will not gratify the desires of the flesh" (Galatians 5:16). It'd be awhile before that message hit home. In the meantime, the light from a liquor store just down the road flashed "Open" through my front window. A half gallon of Popov went for $7.99. I didn't make a lot at the wood-shop, but I could swing that a time or two a week. I told myself that I wouldn't overdo it, wouldn't fall back into the drugs, wouldn't let the old habits take hold again. I was older now. I could drink the loneliness away without losing control.

That's Satan's best lie: "You got this."

Soon I was hitting the bottle every night. Once I fell for the alcohol, cocaine trotted up right behind. Rock offset the downer of booze. Sometimes I couldn't tell you what year it was, but I had no trouble remembering the right balance of chemicals to stay high. It wasn't but a second before I was back in the bowels of addiction.

Drugs filled another need beyond feeding my addictive personality. They gave me a community—people I could party with, people I could talk to and get to know. Drug neighborhoods look alike no matter what city you're in. I'd been to plenty. I knew what they were, and I knew better than to go there. Yet I went anyway. Crack was cheap and plentiful, and the high hit you fast. It didn't take long for me to find a supplier and some friends who were happy to get high with me. I knew where to go to find it, who to meet, and what to say. Even when my regular supplier wasn't around, all I had to do in those neighborhoods was stand on a corner. In minutes, somebody would drive up and ask what I needed. Cash for a foil packet. Just like that you'd made a new friend.

Looking in from the outside, it's easy to say, "Why didn't you walk away? Why didn't you find something else to do, make another group of friends? Why not join a church group, or go to the YMCA, or find other musicians and hang out at coffee shops with them?" It'd be wonderful if those questions had easy answers.

Unless you're an addict, you can't understand the hold drugs have on you. Everybody knows the expression "one day at a time," but those are more than words for us. They're how we stay alive. The addict is always one slip away from the dirty floor of a drug house with a needle in his arm, one weak moment away from being dead before sundown. No matter how long you stay clean, no matter how long you've been sober, the addict knows that tomorrow is not guaranteed. Each day's a battle. Every sober minute's a victory. It gets easier. But it never goes away.

As for music, I took to the street where my songs and talents weren't judged against the youngsters swelling the ranks of country music. Hank hadn't been on the radio in decades. Waylon wasn't in the ground a year before his sound drifted away. But Nashville was full of people who remembered old-time country. They heard it from me when they walked by Forty-Eighth and Charlotte Avenue, or the downtown corners where I'd prop open my guitar case and throw in a five-dollar bill in as a starter. *"You'll be broke but I'll be broker, tonight we're settin' the woods on fire."* I'd play my own songs, throw in some old stuff, add a gospel piece or two, and crowds would gather. Sometimes I'd only get a dollar or two in my case, but most folks were generous.

Like a lot of functioning addicts, I kept a day job, or at least a series of them. I also became manic. A hit or two of cocaine and I'd be up all night doing woodwork with some of the tools I'd bought for the house. For one of my home projects, I bought some maple and cut a head and tail block, and then got some birch plywood to create a form. Then I planed some maple strips to an eighth of an inch and used an iron pipe, propane, and water to bend the wood. It was hard to get it pear shaped, but after some work, the wood started bending just right. Clamps, a dowel, a band saw, a vise, a drill, and about forty hours of labor later, I'd built a mandolin for under a hundred bucks. It was miles from a Gibson, and it probably didn't sound as good as I remember, but the fact that I'd made it caused it to sound richer than anything I could have bought for ten times as much. I loved how it felt in my hands as I'd hammer-on an E and play my interpretation of "In the Pines." *"You caused me to weep, you caused me to mourn. You caused me to leave my home."*

Once again I fell into a predictable routine. I'd work at the woodshop Monday through Friday, and I'd play music on the streets one or two afternoons and evenings a week. Then I'd hit the drugs and booze, especially on the weekends when I could rip it up all night. Soon, I'd let people drift in and out of my house. The right drugs would always buy you a woman for the night. No surprise that none of them filled the lonely hole in my heart.

Before long, I made the jump back to heroin. First I put a little powder on my gums. Then I snorted it. When that took too long, I started mixing it with a little water and putting it in the barrel of a hypodermic needle, or a "work" as the kids called it. I'd tap it to get the air out. Then I'd loop a belt around my arm, put the strap in my mouth, and pull till I saw some veins pop up. The hard part was always sticking yourself. You knew it was gonna sting, but the high was so good you'd do anything to get there. I'd put the needle in at an angle, about twenty degrees, and pull back on the plunger. If you caught a vein, you'd mix a little blood with the milk. Then, I'd push the plunger until my eyes rolled back in my head.

There were times when the very sight of smack excited me so much that I'd wet myself. But I wanted the drug so bad that I'd wait as long as it took, sometimes an hour or more, to shoot up before cleaning myself. That's the power of drugs. That's what they do to you.

Oxy worked when horse wasn't available or money was tight. Grind those pills up and it'd hit your bloodstream fast. Those drugs affect your adrenaline and endorphin levels, things I didn't know or care about at the time. *Euphoria* is the word doctors and counselors use. Folks think that's what the junkie's looking for. Some might be getting high for high's sake, but not many. We're looking for what can't be snorted, or shot, or smoked, or drunk. No counselor or rehab specialist or doctor ever uses the word *peace*. That's what the addict wants. And it ain't ever been found in a foil pouch or a dime bag.

Meth makes your skin wrinkle and your teeth fall out. I

learned that one the hard way. We called it "Tina," which was short for "Christina," which was code for "crystal," which was short for "crystal meth." The first time I lit a pipe of Tina, I thought my heart was gonna explode. But by the time I fell back into it in Nashville, I could tell the good stuff from the cheap imitations. My new "friends" relied on me to make sure we didn't get ripped off.

One girl who was really into chasing meth hits with chilled vodka shots came home with me. I'm ashamed of what we did. I'm ashamed of a lot. And I won't talk about it again until the Lord brings it up at judgment, where I'll have no choice. The only reason to bring it up here is because this girl found out that I had a job, so after she left me in the morning, she put a crew together to rob my house. They took my mandolin, my power tools, and anything else that they could pawn quick or trade for some drugs.

Being victimized sends you through a spin cycle of emotions. I was furious, and then sad, and then depressed. Not that any of that changed how I was living. One weekend after getting paid and spending a good chunk of my check on drugs and alcohol, my house ended up being the gathering spot for a dozen or so addicts, some homeless, but all looking to get high. I played and sang a few songs, drank whiskey, and was the life of the party until I passed out. When I woke up, everybody was gone, and so was my car.

Calling the police wasn't an option. They stole my car because I was too high to notice. My place reeked of whiskey and drugs. Specks of meth dotted my bathtub, and there was blood splattered on the wall near my sink. Empty bottles, dirty needles, wadded sheets, abandoned lighters, flecks of wax paper all over the floor—any cop who showed up would haul me in for running a drug house. So I sat on my front step, put my head in my hands, and tried to breathe without crying.

The cabinet shop where I worked was not close. I asked some of my coworkers to pick me up, and that lasted for a day or two. But the house wasn't on anybody's way to work, and I could only sponge off their generosity for so long. I missed one day for lack of transportation. Then another. And another. I called the first couple of times. I looked up a bus route to see how close it would get me to the woodshop. Not close enough. I got fired.

Bills came by the bushel. The rent went past due first. The power got cut off within a month, and the water went out a week or so after that. A place gets awfully quiet when there isn't even electricity running through the wires. So I packed a pillow, a blanket, a toothbrush, and a couple of changes of clothes into one of those suitcases with wheels on one side. I put my guitar on my back, and I walked down the road, past the liquor store, by my neighbors' places, down to the bus stop. I never looked up—never looked back. I stood there till the bus came. Then I got on and rode into town. Closer to sixty years old than any other round number worth remembering, I was homeless, again, and much in need.

CHAPTER 6

THE ONE WITH HIS EYE ON FAITH

Hitchhiking in the new millennium isn't the adventure that it once was. Adrift and out of money, I played enough on the streets of downtown Nashville to earn the Greyhound fare to New York to see my kids. The bus ride took almost as long as hitching. Between gas, rest stops, and letting people off and on, by the time we rolled into Ithaca I felt like I'd ridden a stagecoach across the country. Once I got there, I wondered why I'd come.

I crashed with some old buddies for a few nights. Then, when the weather warmed up, I slept in a local park for a night or two. There were plenty of public bathrooms where I could bathe. I'd lived up there long enough that friends were willing to help, even though everybody seemed to know that I was drifting. I reconnected and got some help.

Playing the streets was a little strange at first. I'd had a band in Ithaca for so many years that it felt funny setting up near the bus stops and downtown corners near the clubs I'd played in what seemed like a previous life. The crowd had changed. Cornell was bigger, or maybe I'd gotten smaller—it was hard to tell. Either way, young business people still liked hearing a song or two and they'd throw me some cash.

My first phone call with my family didn't go as I'd hoped. Kids don't mean to break your heart, just like you don't mean to break theirs. But being away builds a distance that's more than just miles on a road. I spoke to Leone first, although she didn't speak back much.

"Why are you here?" was about her longest sentence. I didn't tell her right off about being homeless or about losing the car. Best to ease into that kind of news.

I asked when I could see her.

"I don't know," she said. "I'm working."

The call with Jacob didn't go much better. He was quiet, and I could hear the caution in his voice. It was like he was being cross-examined and planned to give the shortest answers possible.

"Could we get together, maybe get a bite to eat?"

"Yeah."

"Any time better than any other?"

"Whatever."

I don't know why I thought it would be different. They'd grown up while I was gone. They had their own lives, and resentments, deep and hard, that my presence rubbed raw. We talked some more and had some meals together, but they'd moved on without me. That cut close to the bone. I thought a lot about my biological dad while I was back up in New York. I wondered what he must have felt when he tried to stay connected to Dave and me. It sure was easy to judge him and to hate him, back when I was young. How could a man walk out on my sweet mother and his two boys, young men who needed him more than he could ever know? That question had swelled and festered for a lot of years.

As I watched Jacob during that trip, the way he tensed up when I hugged him, the way he wouldn't look me square in the eye, and the few times that he did, how he flashed pent-up anger, that question about my dad and our past ricocheted back on me. It sure had been easy to toss every hardship that landed on our family into the "Dad abandoned us" box. That excuse wasn't so easy anymore.

I got a summer job with my old boss in the woodshop and reconnected with some friends. Time has a way of healing. I figured that a few months in a familiar environment, in a routine that brought back memories, might make things better for everybody.

Then the bottom fell out. Leone started to wonder about her heritage. Was she Irish? Was she Italian? German? A little of everything? I sure couldn't give her any details, and Lynn wasn't much better on the family-history front. DNA tests had become all the rage with young adults, so she found a company and sent off a swab or two to find out what she could. The results turned everything upside down. She found me and screamed, "How could you not tell me?"

"Tell you what?" I had no idea what could have made her this upset.

"You're not my father. All this time I've had a dad out there somewhere, and I thought all I had was you."

My head spun and I couldn't catch my breath. I wanted to say that I had no idea, that all of this was news to me, but I wasn't sure how she'd take that. Lynn and I had been wild as wolves when we were together, breaking up and getting back together so often it's amazing we stayed married as long as we did. But I never suspected that Leone wasn't my daughter. If I had known, it wouldn't have changed how much I loved her. Fathering a child is a lot more than a couple of seconds of pleasure and a drop or two of DNA. That's the least of it. If I had known, I would have done whatever it took to make sure she was my daughter under the law, since she always had been and always would be in my heart. No matter what I thought of her mother and what she'd done, I wanted Leone to know that being her father was the best thing that had happened to me, regardless of what some DNA test said. I wanted to tell her all of that, but I was too shocked to speak. She stormed away, crying.

I called Lynn immediately. "I know why you'd do this to me, but why would you do it to your daughter?" I asked.

"I didn't want to hurt her," she said.

"That's the kind of thing that'll affect her for the rest of her life," I told her. "Finding out this way . . . Oh, Lord."

I tried to behave as though the news didn't turn me upside down, and as far as my feelings for Leone went, it didn't. I was her father, regardless of who got her mother pregnant. She didn't see it that way and went looking for her "real dad," as she called him. That put me back in the bottom of a bottle, trying everything I could to kill the pain.

My routine soured. Summer turned to fall and the wood-shop slowed down. Early September, when the kids came back to college, I could play the streets and pick up an odd job here and there, but that didn't last long. My heart wasn't into it once the chill hit the air. The situation with Leone weighed hard, so I tried to lighten the load by getting drunk. Bus fare to Nashville ran about eighty bucks. With food and a fifth of vodka, the trip back cost about 150 dollars, which left me just enough from my last paycheck to pick up a couple of hits of crack when I hit my old West Nashville neighborhoods.

My first two nights back in Tennessee were spent on the floor of a drug house surrounded by candy wrappers, dried dog feces, plastic bottles, and an empty Campbell's soup can. There was a stained mattress with no sheets in a corner, but it was usually taken by somebody. A girl was there the first night with dried blood that had run from her nose to the mattress to the floor. I didn't check to see if she was breathing. She was gone the next day. What was left of my clothes, which wasn't much, was dirty, so I went to a street corner and flew a cardboard flag for a few hours. Five bucks was enough to hit the Laundromat and make bus fare into downtown.

The Nashville Rescue Mission was a brick-and-glass building that could pass for a basketball arena except for the big heart logo with a cross in the middle. The motto was "Hope Lives Here." For a good long spell, I did too. I played on the downtown streets for drug money. I rode the city bus back out to Charlotte Avenue, where I'd hang out at the library during the day—a place where a lot of homeless people gathered to stay warm in the winter, catch a quiet nap in one of the reading chairs, and get on the Internet at one of the public computers. It was also close to a couple of the Interstate 40 exit ramps, so you could wander out there with a cardboard sign explaining your plight and asking for help. Nobody called it begging, because that's not what any of us thought. I never pleaded with a stranger for money. I'd politely ask if he could spare a little, but that was it. If the person said no or ignored me, I'd let it go, sometimes even offering a "God bless you," as he walked away. That wasn't sarcasm. I wanted God to bless everybody.

Most people don't understand how I could fall into the homeless life so easy, because they've never lived it. I'd been there so much of my life that I barely knew different. Even when I had a place, I would often fall into a homeless way of living. I once went down to Charlotte, North Carolina, to visit my brother Dave. He'd married Maryann DeVito, whose father owned a cesspool business on Long Island. Dave had worked on her dad's trucks up there, and Maryann, who was younger, had a crush on Dave before they hooked up. They had a son, and

Dave got a body shop job near the Charlotte Motor Speedway. Maryann didn't care much for me, so when I hitchhiked down to see my brother, I didn't want to cause trouble by staying at his house. I went downtown and looked for a shelter or a YMCA. Everything was full, so I broke into an empty warehouse where I found tons of packing foam. I made a bed out of that, used a box as a cover, and got a great night's sleep before putting a thumb in the air and heading home. That sort of thing had been common throughout my life. When I fell into homelessness in Nashville, it was like going back to what I knew, back to the places and the mind-set where I was comfortable.

At times homelessness sharpens you. Not knowing where you're gonna sleep, or what you're gonna eat, or who you're gonna run into from one day to the next keeps you on your toes. Nothing's routine, so you gotta stay alert. I feel like my powers of observation, the window into human nature that I still have today, came from my time on the street. I could watch a businessman walk out of a restaurant in the afternoon and know whether he'd had lunch with his wife, his mistress, a client, or his business partner. And I could tell how the meal went. I could stand near the gas station and tell you who was driving to a nightclub, who was going to work, who was headed home, and who was heading out of town for good. When your day is spent outside watching people, you pick up little cues. How a man holds his shoulders, how he rocks back and forth on his toes, how a woman looks at the ground, the lines on her forehead or around her mouth: they all speak to what's going on inside. I got good at hearing that language.

———

Observation is the broth of all songwriting. I watched a lot of folks for more hours than I could count, and I got some great material from it. 'Course, I didn't use it all. I was too busy getting high most nights to write good music. I know a lot of musicians say that they wrote this or that song when they were stoned. Artists talk like that a lot. I heard Mick Jagger talking once about recording *Sticky Fingers*, and how much dope they all smoked while doing it. Problem is, that album ain't great because of the drugs. It's great in spite of the drugs. Nobody plays music better high. Nobody writes clearer when they're drunk or stoned. The talent and discipline to be an artist isn't magically brought out by artificial substances. It's a blessing from God. When you dull it with booze or barbiturates, you tarnish the gift and disrespect the Giver.

Eating was another adventure. Dumpster diving has never been a problem for me. I'd been doing that since I was a kid. Me and Dave used to look at it like a treasure hunt. We'd get excited when we'd find an old lawn chair somebody threw out, an old pipe that we could bend into a frame, or a piece of wire, which we could find a million ways to use. Dumpsters were grab bags, opportunities to show off, to find good use for what other folks considered junk.

Jumping in there to get a bite to eat wasn't a bother at all, especially when you realize that the dumpsters near restaurants and grocery stores toss out entire untouched meals. As long as it hadn't been contaminated, I had no problem pulling good food out of the garbage. It felt great. I believed that I was keeping it from going to waste. I never got bit while I was in there, but I ran up on some king-sized rats. Some of 'em were bigger than the alley cats that hung out behind every restaurant in town. You never get used to turning over a box and having a rat bare its teeth and hiss at you. Something about the way they look jolts you. One thing about it, though: you lose your appetite right quick after you see one. That's what separates the poor in America from other parts of the world. No homeless person I know would fight a rat for food in a dumpster. In India and parts of Asia and Africa, folks would eat the food and the rat. In that respect, we do live in the land of milk and honey.

Food at the mission was better than you could want. Volunteers came in every day to serve hot meals. Not only was it a great way to get some excellent, healthy meat and vegetables, you always met interesting people. Most of the volunteers were Christians who signed up to serve through their church, but we also had rabbis, civic leaders, and people who weren't affiliated with religion at all. They all enjoyed talking. Very few of 'em asked how we'd ended up living on the street. I guess they didn't want to run any of us off by being nosy. A time or two, after you got to know a fella, you might volunteer to tell your story. They were eager to hear it, in part because they were curious about the ins and outs of a life they could never imagine. But they were also earnest in wanting to help.

You couldn't really get deep with 'em. A man who's lived his whole life in a stable home with an intact family, a fella who's gone to the right college and always had a job, that guy cannot figure out how anybody could end up on the street. He sees homelessness as being like hunger in Africa or a lack of drinking water in Mexico: it's a nagging problem that seems, to him at least, to have an easy solution. You get a job, find an apartment, move in with family . . . whatever it is the fella looking in from the outside would do if he had a tidal wave of bad things happen to him. But what that fella don't realize is the homeless person don't see living on the street as a big problem. Most folks I know from the street weren't torn up about being there. They would have appreciated having a room someplace, but the weight of having an apartment or a house—the responsibilities of paying rent and keeping the lights on, as well as the feeling of being tied to one location—makes a wandering person nervous. What the man volunteering at the shelter—looking in on us like we're some rare, exotic birds that need to be rescued from the wild—don't get is that when you have no home, everywhere is your home.

I ain't advocating for homelessness. There are too many kids living without a stable address, and way too many folks with mental problems living on the streets. But that guy who spends an hour a month volunteering in the soup kitchen who sees homelessness as a problem in need of a couple of quick fixes doesn't know the people he's feeding.

If there's one quick and easy fix to homelessness, it's love your neighbor as a brother in Christ, even when he smells, even when he's lost his teeth, even when he eats out of a dumpster and sleeps in the back seat of a junk car. Love him when he's homeless in the richest country in the history of the world.

———

—

'Course, my reason for being in that mission didn't change. While I didn't mind homelessness, and felt right comfortable sleeping wherever nightfall landed me, I'd gotten there because drugs and alcohol controlled my life. Whenever I got a little money, either by playing on the street or flying a cardboard flag at an exit ramp, my priority was a couple of crackers (street slang for crack) or a juice joint (a marijuana joint sprinkled with crack). Food, shelter, and clothing all came later. The mission wouldn't let you in if you carried contraband, so if I'd scored a hit or two, I'd roam between what you'd call crack houses. They were my friends' places that happened to be where drugs were sold and used, and where addicts sometimes crashed.

By that time, I'd learned a whole new language. *P-funk* was crack and PCP smoked together; *base*, *gum*, *candy*, and *balls* all referred to crack; *sheetrock* was a mix of crack and LSD; and *snowcaps* were prime stuff—cocaine sprinkled over marijuana bong hits. *Ludes*, *crank*, *tar*, *O*, and *ex* hadn't changed in decades. Neither had the word *junkie*, which is what I'd become.

One day I dove in a dumpster and, after sifting through some soggy cardboard, rotten cantaloupe, and black lettuce, I found an old tent, which was like striking gold. There's some woods off Fifty-Fourth Street near Sylvan Park down by Richland Creek. They got a golf course nearby. But just north of that are some lowlands. I put that tent up and lived there a good long while until the cops ran me in for vagrancy. Then I lived in jail, eating county food, making new friends, and getting sober.

—

Most of the people in local lockup were there on drug charges, so we had a lot in common. The clang of a cell door no longer jarred me. I found it soothing. It was an opportunity to meet new people, clear my head, get some hot food, and maybe make another contact or two for drugs when we got out.

When I was released from that stint, the tent was gone. So I wandered to the other side of the highway and found a dry culvert behind a Walmart near the Cumberland River. That made for a great house. Walmart threw out a king's load of stuff. I found an old mattress behind an apartment complex, along with a blanket and some hardware, which was perfect. I hauled all of that into that culvert. Cool and quiet, its only problems were the smells mixing out of the river and restaurants and the fact that you got washed out every time it rained. Snakes wriggled down there in the summertime, and any food I brought was bound to attract rats. But the cops left you alone down there. That became home for quite a few months until the weather turned and I had to haul it back to the mission to keep from freezing to death.

Between the culvert and the nearest library stood a wood-shop called Cliff's Cabinet Company. I stopped in there and met the owners, an African American couple named John and Penny Combs. I told 'em the good parts of my story, leaving out what I couldn't bring myself to say aloud. They knew I had some darkness, some battles I'd likely lose in the days ahead. They hired me despite the fact that I didn't have an address. The Combses were another gift from God, a pair of angels put in front of me at exactly the right time. All I had to do was embrace 'em.

Penny asked me about my music, probably because I took my guitar with me everywhere I went. You couldn't just leave something like that lying around, even in the mission. It'd have been gone, for sure. Penny didn't pry, but she knew how to ask the right questions. *Have you written any songs lately? When are you going to audition for another music job? Did you hear about the open-mic night down the road? Have you ever thought about playing at charity events?* This wasn't an inquisition; it was Penny nudging me where she knew I needed to go. If it hadn't've been for the drugs, I'd have listened closer. But when all you can think about is getting off work so you can cash your paycheck and find the nearest dealer, a lot of things slip by you. I think John and Penny recognized my affliction. They'd likely seen it before.

I didn't tell 'em much about my living arrangements. There were a couple of I-40 overpasses at Forty-Eighth and Fifty-Second Streets. The bridges were high enough that you had a concrete slab at about a thirty-degree angle sloping up about thirty-five feet, just far enough that a fella who camped out on the flat area, about six feet wide and five feet from the bottom of the bridge, couldn't be seen from down below. You'd have to climb all the way up to find whoever was there, and that was no easy feat. The Tennessee Department of Transportation put up fences to keep people like me from climbing up there, but a snip here and there with a tin shear and you could make a gate to both platforms. It was the perfect spot to crash when the floors of the drug houses were taken and I was carrying too much dope to get a cot at the shelter.

———

Folks don't figure a homeless person to be employed. The reason you're homeless is you don't work, or so people think. But you'd be stunned how many people on the streets have some sort of employment. They're dishwashers, janitors, and yardmen. When you see a restaurant hiring a forty-year-old to wash dishes and mop the kitchen floor, where do you think he's living? Those men and women pulling weeds off the side of the road or mowing the pretty entrance to the gated community, where do you reckon they lay their heads at night? Some have places, cheap apartments with roommates or with a spouse who also works. More than you'd think are wanderers. They get a couch or a spare room with a buddy, drift from drug house to drug house, or sleep in the shelters. I was a cabinetmaker during most of my homeless years in Nashville.

There was a paycheck-cashing place within walking distance of Cliff's Cabinets, which wasn't too far from the overpasses where I spent many a summer night. In between those two overpasses, near a Shell gas station with a working bathroom that had hot water and a liquid soap dispenser, stood the West Nashville United Methodist Church, a stone-and-brick building that smelled of antiseptic cleaner and anointing oil. In the basement they had a food mission called the Little Pantry That Could, run by another of my guardian angels, a woman named Stacy Downey, who would make sure I'd eaten at least one fruit and vegetable a day. The pantry always had the best canned food, and Stacy always knew where I could get some decent clothes. If I needed socks or a new pair of jeans, Stacy wouldn't let me leave until I was outfitted.

———

Like Penny Combs, Stacy would always ask about my music. She'd sometimes ask me to play outside the church. I'd strike up a song or two and usually draw a little crowd, mostly other home- less people in the pantry. Occasionally somebody would come out of the church to listen. A few times folks who were donating items wandered out. I didn't pay much attention to who was there. Any crowd was a good one. After I'd finish, Stacy would say, "You've got a gift, Doug. God given. Use it well."

I'd thank her, but I usually couldn't wait to get away to find my next high.

The thing about homelessness is how long life goes without any distinguishing events. One day bleeds into the next with no graduations to attend or retirements to celebrate, no new movies or plays to talk about at the water cooler, and no trips to plan. I got up, sometimes at the mission and sometimes outside, and if I was carrying, I'd pop a little wake-up, which is street slang for snorting cocaine first thing in the morning. Then I'd go to the cabinet shop when there was work.

Penny and John had to lay me off some, not because of stuff I'd done (although they'd have been well within reason to put a druggie on the road, no matter how good he was with a table saw), but because, like every other construction-based business, cabinet work had its ups and downs. Every time they had to lay me off, I thought Penny was gonna cry. More than once I ended up comforting her, telling her that I'd be fine. She always made me promise to check in every couple of weeks and they'd hire me back as soon as they could. Good to her word, as soon as business picked up, I was back at work in the shop.

Weeks, months, seasons, years came and went. Weekends were busy downtown. Between Vanderbilt sports teams, the Titans, the Predators, and the concerts and stuff, you could always find a crowd milling around. I'd throw my case open and play some songs to make a few bucks, but nothing big or dramatic.

Sometimes the dealers in the drug neighborhoods I'd visit would up and vanish. A day or two later, I'd hear something about a shooting. I didn't pay attention. I didn't want to hear that stuff. Socializing never got too deep in those neighborhoods because there was a lot of stuff you didn't want to talk about and even more stuff you didn't want to hear. I'd partied with some people for years without ever knowing their real names, where they were from, or anything about 'em other than what kind of drugs and music they liked. After so many years in the bottom of a bottle or the short end of a crack pipe, your biology changes. You can't hold a thought or a memory for more than a minute or two, and you react to stuff a lot different than you did before. If somebody started an argument, I'd overreact and either get out of there or jump in the middle of it, ready to fight to the death. There was no in-between. No calming things down. My fight-or-flight reflexes were full throttle all the time. Even a small disagreement, something that shouldn't set a guy off, would send me into a tailspin. But things that should have upset me—a buddy from the neighborhood going to prison for dealing, or a woman I knew selling her body for the next hit of horse—those rolled off me like they were nothing.

One afternoon, as I sat outside a drug house waiting on a

buddy to get home, a guy in a pickup truck pulled up and said, "What do you need?"

I said, "Crack cocaine and a woman."

"I'll be right back," he said.

He delivered both.

———

She was thin, not in a healthy way, but beautiful, and she had a lot of spunk, which attracted me to her even more. Her name was Angela, sometimes Angie, and she was wild as a goat in heat. From the moment I saw her she wanted to party, and I was all too happy to oblige. We spent the night together in a drug house, high and seeking some happiness. The next morning she walked away. I called out, "Don't leave." But she just raised her hand over her head and waved without looking back. "At least give me your number," I said. She wouldn't do that, either. I was convinced she was gone.

A few weeks later, still homeless and splitting time between the drug houses, the bridges, and the shelter, I went to another friend's house to smoke crack, and, lo and behold, there she was again, already high as a rocket and tripping out on a dirty couch.

"Hey, Angela, it's me, Doug," I said.

She grabbed me by the neck and kissed me hard. We were together pretty regular after that.

Except we really weren't. It's hard to admit what either of us did, but she was with other men for money and drugs. We got together the way most street people do: I would be standing out on a corner holding a cardboard sign, trying to raise enough money to get high, and I would see her riding by in a car with another guy. Jealousy wasn't in us. We were so deep in dependency that normal, moral behavior didn't apply. The feelings that a man would have if he saw his girl with another man, knowing what was happening between them—drugs dulled that in both of us. We were in a downward spiral without realizing it. I'd see her with another guy and think, *Oh, I hope she comes back and finds me.* An hour or so later, she'd appear out of nowhere. We'd take whatever money we'd both raised and buy more drugs.

One night we were together under the bridge. The rumbling of the traffic was light and it wasn't too cold out. No rats bothered us, so we got a good night's sleep. When I woke up, I saw Angie with a piece of cardboard sweeping the ledge, shoving beer cans, broken bottles, trash, and grime down the concrete bank.

"Angie, why are you cleaning up?" I asked. "We're under a bridge. This ain't a house."

She smiled and said, "This is our house."

That's when I knew she was the girl for me. Sometimes we'd wake up and walk down to a home owned by a saintly old man named Charlie Wright who would care for prostitutes who needed a place to get away from the street. Angie would cook breakfast for us at Charlie's before we'd start our day. Sometimes that was me going to the woodshop. Other times, when woodwork was light or I'd been laid off, we'd head out to the street where I'd either play music for tips or put up a sign asking for money.

Other mornings we'd go to a dumpster where I'd dig around and find a Styrofoam cup. Then I'd go into the restroom at a gas station or fast-food place and fill the cup with liquid soap. Me and Angie would walk down to the creek, take our clothes off, bathe, and wash our clothes in the open water. We'd lie next to our clothes and each other so we'd dry in the sun. Then we'd get dressed and walk to the dumpster behind Papa John's Pizza. There was always a full pie in there. I'd get the pizza, and we'd walk to Kroger, where they had free coffee in the deli. We'd sit on the patio furniture they were trying to sell out front, eat our pizza, and drink our coffee without a care in the world.

We were together for two years, but not all the time. I stayed in the mission some. During that time, a few opportunities came my way, but I wasn't in a position in my life to take advantage of them. One day I was playing on the street near the mission when a guy I'd met before named Jeff Scarborough, who worked in a building across the street, walked up to me and said, "I have a guy who wants to record some of your songs."

I said, "I don't have the money for anything like that."

But he said, "No, no, I took him a tape of the stuff you do out here on the street. He wants you to come to his studio so he can lay some tracks down for you."

He gave me the card of a fellow named Brian Irwin at Monster Studios in East Nashville. By that point, like a lot of homeless people in America, I had a cell phone, so I called Brian. He asked me to come out.

I caught a bus to East Nashville and walked about half a mile to Monster Studios, where Brian brought me in and listened to what I thought were my five best songs. He played some backup, and we worked out some stuff. Then he said, "Let's get you recorded."

We laid down five tracks. Brian would later pay to have a hundred copies of an EP made for me. It was a level of kindness I didn't deserve, but one I recognized as being inspired by a higher power. That was also when I learned a lot about the modern recording process, information that would serve me well once God was ready to use me in the highest way.

Another incident of unnatural kindness came when Penny Combs offered to have me make the cabinets for Glen Hardin, who had played piano with Elvis and John Denver.

"You mean that Glen Hardin?" I asked.

"Yes, he needs new cabinets," Penny said. "I thought you might like to meet him. Would you like the job?"

"You bet. Thank you, Penny. That's wonderful."

I met Hardin, who was a very nice fella. But rather than use this blessing as motivation, or a springboard, I looked at Glen's nice home, and all the records on the wall, and it reminded me of what I'd once dreamed about, what I thought the life of a country artist should be. I finished the job as quick as possible and never went back.

Me and Angie fell into a routine of our own, although it's not what anybody would call conventional. I'd stay at the mission Monday through Friday and work at Cliff's Cabinets. She'd work the streets in ways I don't want to think about and won't talk about again. On Friday night, we'd hook up and hit the nearest drug house, where we'd spend the weekend getting high and doing as many illicit things as possible. I'd head back to the mission on Sunday night, sober up, and start the process over.

My brother Dave died during that time. Doctors said he'd inhaled too many fumes from the body shops. It was a mournful period, but I wasn't moved enough by Dave's passing to change my way of life. He'd been sober for fifteen years and had turned his life into something worth copying—a nice house and a family that loved him, a good reputation in town, and a group of sorrowful friends to grieve for him when he was gone. If I'd had my wits, I would have seen God's handwriting on all of that. But I wasn't quite there. Not yet.

———

While we were together, I wrote a song about Angie called "Burning a Hole in My Pocket."

> *The way you do the things you do*
> *eating my heart out with your eyes*
> *The way you make me feel so young*
> *walking around mesmerized*
> *You lit a torch in my soul*
> *like a Chinese bottle rocket*
> *Oh, Angie, my sweet thing*
> *burning a hole in my pocket.*

It was upbeat and fun and could be a little jazzy if somebody wanted to play it that way. That song summed up my bright days with Angie, and there were plenty of 'em. Looking in from the outside, it's hard to understand how two people living under bridges and eating out of dumpsters or off the charity of others could be so jolly. But we were as happy a pair as you'd find when we were together. But like all good feelings born in sin, there was a price to pay. It turned out to be a big one.

Angie left me for a younger man who had a car and a permanent address. At first I thought it'd be okay, like the men she was with other times. She'd come back to me once she got some cash and maybe a few things out of him. But that ain't how it worked out. She'd still come around some to get high, but that was it. We weren't together. We didn't talk like we did before. We didn't stay together. What we'd had, like what I'd had with Lynn, vanished in a cloud of blue smoke. It ate me up to the point where I'd follow her and write her notes telling her how much I loved her, telling her how heartbroken I was by what'd happened. In practical terms, I was a stalker, although I never thought of it that way. I never would have harmed a soul, but her new man didn't know that.

The two of them got married pretty quick, and he came to me and said, "I don't want you writing love letters to my wife. It's not right."

He was right about that. So I wrote a couple of songs. The first, "Angie's Song," was a plea:

Let me be the one who mails you a vote of
confidence, while you're laying there in jail

Let me be the one who cries and moans to the
    hanging judge, gotta get my Baby some bail
Let me be the one who watches you from a
    distance, every Friday night
Let me be the one who takes down your pusher
    man, when you finally lose your appetite
Let me be the one who walks down to the liquor
    store, somebody else tonight
Let me be the one who gets down on his hands
    and knees and thanks God that you're alright
Gonna be alright, Baby.

Later on in the song, I wrote:

Let me be the one with his eye on his faith, cause
    he knows God can fix anything
Let me be the one who shares His love and His
    grace, making a joyful noise when I sing.

I was hell-deep in addiction when those words first came out of me. But my rock bottom was close at hand.

My addiction got so bad that I started driving the getaway car for some guys who were robbing truckers. I would pull up to a truck stop, the guys would find a truck where the driver was inside getting dinner or something, and they'd rifle through the back, grabbing whatever they could. By keeping my head turned, not looking at their thieving, I told myself I wasn't a part of it. I told myself I wasn't stealing. I bragged that I'd never stole, even in the worst of my abuse. That was how far from reality my mind had gone. Those boys stole everything from cigarettes to stereos, and even though I was neck-deep in it with them, somehow I thought that if I didn't actually take the stuff, didn't actually watch them breaking into someone else's property and breaking one of God's earliest commandments, that I wasn't a thief just like 'em. 'Course, when they hopped back in the car, we'd take whatever they got directly to the dealers so we could trade it in for drugs. I didn't have any trouble with that part of the transaction.

Drugs rob you of your good sense. It's a miracle I've got any left.

Those truck robberies would have landed me in prison for a long stretch. As it was, my last stint in jail was like my first in that I went in for something I didn't do. Me and Angie, who still came out to get high with me after she started seeing her eventual husband, were firing up a pipe behind Saint Ann Catholic Church. The parking lot was buffered by trees, so it was quiet—a great place to get high. Irony runs right past you when you're tweaking. Just a few feet from the altar, a crucifix displayed above, all we could think about was smoking crack.

Well, Angie had a reaction and started seizing. Fell to the ground, head banging on the concrete, flailing around, hitting the fence. I held her still as best I could till she came out of it. Then she got up and started to stumble away. I called after her, but I was too high to stop her. She went back to her then-boyfriend's place, who didn't like her being anywhere near me. When he saw how banged up she was, he took her to the hospital. Any time a drug case comes in, especially where injuries are involved, doctors call the cops. The police took a keen interest in the cuts and bruises, especially when her friend said, "Doug Seegers did that to her."

I was known to the cops, so it didn't take long for me to be hauled in for battery. I told 'em exactly what happened, but they weren't interested. After a day in jail, a public defender came to me with a deal. If I pled guilty, I'd get probation and be out that day. If I didn't, I'd be in jail till trial.

A man with more fight in him would've stood up, especially being accused of hitting a woman. But dope and booze pull all that out of you. I took the deal and was back on the street before sundown. That didn't seem like a hard choice at all. I was high again by nightfall.

Problem was, the deal included not getting arrested again. When you're homeless, trespassing and vagrancy are your everyday address. So I got run up for trespassing and caught a judge who had no use for batterers. He gave me six months in county. I wound up doing four and a half of the hardest months of my life. Not only did I miss the drugs, but I was in for something I didn't do, which made each day feel like stolen time.

I didn't realize at the time that it was my fault. Even though I never raised my hand to Angela, and never would have, I was the one who took the deal. Nobody else. I'm the one who said I did something that I did not do. I took the shortcut. I lied. And I paid the price.

Once I got out, I went right back to my old ways. After one particularly bad night, I climbed down from beneath the

Forty-Eighth Street overpass about nine in the morning, my head down as I shuffled along the grass bank. I was hungover and hungry, ready to start the cycle anew. I crawled through the little makeshift gate I'd cut in the fence. That's when I stood up and ran headlong into Stacy Downey, who was walking to work at the Little Pantry That Could. The sadness on her face hit me like a board.

"Oh, Stacy, I'm sorry you saw me like this," I said. "Please don't tell anyone."

Her lips put on a tight smile, but her eyes looked like they could flood at any second. "It's our secret," she said.

I went down to the Richland Creek to wash, alone. Later that day, I sat down and wrote a song.

> *I'm going down to the river*
> *   to wash my soul again*
> *I've been runnin' with the Devil,*
> *   and I know he's not my friend*
> *I've been falling by this wayside,*
> *   livin' in this world of sin*
> *I'm going down to the river,*
> *   gonna wash my soul again*

———

The Bible says, "The wages of sin is death" (Romans 6:23). I believe that. But I also believe that most people read it wrong. They think of God pointing a finger of judgment down on you,

———

threating to kill you if you sin. That's not it at all. It's a plea, like a parent saying, "Don't put your hand in that fire" or "Don't run with that knife."

Sin kills your conscience. Things that you know ought to bother you—things like a buddy getting shot or a girlfriend turning tricks with other men—somehow they don't mean nothing. Things you know better than to do, things you know are wrong, things that would have gnawed at you before—like driving a getaway car or saying you hit somebody when you didn't just so you can get out of a predicament and get high again—you do those things anyway, and you do 'em without so much as a second thought. Things come out of your own mouth that would have made you flinch if you'd heard 'em as a young man. You do things that, if you'd seen them being done before, would have given you the shivers.

Sin kills your marriage, taking away the deep bond between two people that God's blessed. It kills how you get on with your kids, forever tainting their thinking about you. It kills the truth, and you caring about it. It kills the feelings of intimacy that a man ought to have with his bride, the feelings of anticipation that you ought to have when a friend smiles at you. It kills your love of little things like a child's laugh or a glowing sunrise. Sin kills the sadness you should feel when others are wronged.

Sin kills shame.

That's what "wages of sin" means. God's not scolding you. He's loving you.

CHAPTER 7

RESTORATION SOON

S alvation can come anywhere. Emperors have found God in palaces, and slaves have found him in chains. He came to me on a slab of broken concrete, weeds stretching up between the cracks, fighting for sunlight in a corner full of darkness.

The day had been like most. I woke up with a thick head and a deep hunger. Food and vodka were my first and only thoughts. So I stumbled out of where I was staying, grabbed a sandwich at McDonald's, and was the first person in the door when the liquor store opened. I paid with wadded bills and some change I'd gotten from strangers. Armed with a half gallon of Smirnoff, I walked to an old parking lot behind the Catholic church, one that needed repaving. A chain-link fence stretched across the back. What had once been white concrete had aged to varying shades of brown. It bulged and buckled where roots from nearby trees had tunneled underneath. Vines tangled up on the fence so light had a hard time creeping through, even on a clear day.

My hands shook, but I knew that would stop once I cracked the seal and took a gulp or two. My head would feel better too. The muscles in my shoulders and neck quivered and tensed. They'd turn loose once the vodka took hold. I'd be warm then, and numb soon enough.

By now I was sixty-three years old, a solid fifteen years into the Nashville experiment. My joints had held up good even if my mind and my will had faltered. It took longer to straighten my knees in the cold, but I didn't have trouble walking. Stairs didn't bother me when I was sober. But my kidneys gave me trouble, and I'd get a burning pain in my gut sometimes when I ate. Sleeping outside, it's a wonder I didn't get double pneumonia, but my lungs felt okay. My heart fluttered more than it should, but a few deep breaths and a little walk always cleared that up.

This morning my heart didn't jump like a lot of times when I got a bottle. If anything, I felt heavy. I sat down and leaned back on the fence. The vines kinda hid me, which I liked. A man knows he's in the wrong when his instincts are to hide what he's doing. That was me with drugs and alcohol. I didn't mind being out front with my guitar, homeless or not. I didn't slink away from the mission, and I wasn't embarrassed to ask for help on the street. Being homeless wasn't an embarrassment. But when I was getting high, I slipped out of sight, most times without thinking about it.

I could taste the liquor and feel the burn in my throat before I opened the bottle. It wasn't something I wanted. I needed it. The thought of diving into another drink didn't excite me. It made me sad. I'd come to Tennessee to start a new life, to give the musician in me room to grow up. I'd come here to reach the top. Instead, I was as low as a man could go. I'd lost my dentures, so I kept pulling my upper lip down, waiting on the vodka. Every nerve tingled. It was like every part of my body was bouncing like school kids waiting on the final bell. A small voice in the back of my mind, so faint I could barely make it out over all the shouting to get that bottle open, asked: *Where is that man who drove down here with a notebook full of songs? What happened to that fella who left his home hot on the trail of a dream? What became of that guy who was going to make a name for himself in Nashville?*

Cravings for an addict are more than just longing for a taste or being anxious for a high. Your cells react to the drink. I could feel my blood rising as my fingers rubbed on that bottle. Glands in the back of my throat swelled up waiting on the burn. My tongue rolled just the way it would if I was pulling on a bottle. I could feel my spit evaporate like rain on a hot roof. I'd gulp this one like a sprinter chugs water.

I don't know what compelled me to do it, but at that very moment, I looked up and saw the sun flicker across the windows of the Catholic church, rays dancing like fairies. Bright winks. The sunlight tapped against my eyes. A gentle knock. Me and Dave used to flick light at each other with bits of broken mirror we'd find down at the beach. We'd pretend we knew Morse code and were sending signals to each other. I remembered feeling almost hypnotized by the sunlight when it bounced toward me thata way. The Methodist church in Babylon used to have windows that reflected the rays like that too. Sometimes as a child I'd jump and reach for them, as if I could catch a beam of light. That's when something I'd never thought about before hit me like a board to the head, and anguish washed over me like a flood.

If I was to die right here in this parking lot, who'd find me? Who'd notice that I was gone? Who'd miss me? I couldn't come up with a good answer. Maybe somebody coming to work would run up on my body. Maybe another homeless person would stumble across me and realize that I wasn't passed out. Or maybe I'd lay right here till my carcass bloated and started to stink. No matter what, I'd most likely be cremated at county expense before any of my angels knew I was gone. Stacy Downey at the Little Pantry That Could, Penny Combs at Cliff's Cabinets, the other saints whose paths I crossed so often—like Reverend Becca Stevens, who created Magdalene Ministries and the Thistle Stop Café, a coffee shop where former prostitutes could work while putting their lives back together, which was within sight of the lot where I sat; or Charlie Wright, who opened his home and fed people like me and Angie and any other streetwalkers who stumbled along.

Then there were the kind souls who worked at the Nashville Rescue Mission, who fed me and kept me warm in the winter, who made sure I had a blanket at night and a cup of coffee in the morning. None of those folks would know anything about my demise until it was too late. I'd be identified by my finger-prints. Lord knows I'd been in the system enough. Somebody'd reach out to my kids, eventually. Jacob would be the easiest to find. He had a job and a phone, or at least he did when I'd last heard from him. It'd been a while since we spoke. I could only imagine how the call would go: *Mister Seegers, we're sorry to inform you that your father drank himself to death alone in an empty parking lot. We don't know much else.*

My little brother would find out somehow, but not in time. I'd be burned to ashes and buried in a pauper's grave by the time my family and friends knew I was gone. There'd be bitter tears, but not many, and not for the reasons anybody'd want.

My music, my life, the love I had to give—everything I'd hoped to do, every person I'd hoped to touch, it would all van-ish. I'd been on the earth six decades. Had I done anything to leave it better than the day I was born? Had I made a difference, big or small, in my corner of the universe? I've always believed that every life has a purpose—that every person plays a part in God's grand plan. Unfortunately, some folks' purpose is to set a bad example. The Lord don't want it that way. He wants one and all to walk with him. But those who don't, those who fall short, remind others that there's a standard of perfection, one that could not have been set by men. If men had come up with the idea of perfect, we'da kept lowering the bar to suit ourownselves. That king over there, he's a pretty good dude, so whatever he does, let's call it "perfect," even if he had thirty-five wives and didn't give two hoots about most of his daughters. That reverend who led those people in Africa to declare their independence, to start their own country and govern theirown-selves, he looked perfect enough by men's standards. Let's call whatever he did perfect, even though he looked the other way at violence and corruption, and even took some loot hisownself.

Because we know in our hearts that we haven't measured up to perfect, we also know, deep down, even if we have a hard time admitting it, that the standard we reach for without ever being able to grab it had to have been set by a higher, unseen power. That's how we know God's real. He is perfect. And he lets us know that perfect is out there and we ought to try to reach it. We also feel his disappointment when we fall short.

I looked at the sunlight flashing off those church windows like a beacon or the light on top of a police car. Suddenly, I was struck by the darkness in my own corner. It hadn't always been this way. I'd often walked to church with Mom and Grandma and thought how bright the world seemed. But it wasn't an outside light. The brightness was what I felt in me. It was a brightness that I somehow knew glowed inside all of us—a light you couldn't see, and a warmth that was better than fire. Where had that feeling gone? How would a fella get it back? Was it something you outgrew? Or was it available to everyone—young and old, man and woman, rich and dirt-poor homeless?

As I looked at that Catholic church with its gray stones and arched doorways, my mind flashed back to a story I'd learned while sitting in those pews on Long Island with Dave. I wasn't sure about the actual words, but I remembered the gist. A Samaritan woman goes to a well on a mountain. It's a brutal hot day and she's carrying a water jar. Jesus is resting and asks her for water. She says something like, "You're a Jew and I'm a Samaritan. That's like the Hatfields and McCoys. We're not supposed to talk, much less share a drink together." That part always struck me. Some people wouldn't talk to me at times because I was homeless, or poor, or I wasn't their kind. But Jesus talked to her. He asked her to go home and get her husband so he could tell them both that he was the Messiah.

She said, "I don't got a husband."

Jesus said, "I know. You've had five, and you're not married to the man you're living with now."

He knew she'd made a mess of her life. She was the equivalent of a modern-day prostitute who'd sell her body for the next hit, or an alcoholic who'd let booze ruin every relationship. She was the crack addict you wouldn't speak to on a bet or the homeless person you'd walk to the other side of the street to avoid. But Jesus didn't say, "Be gone, woman" or "Nope, sorry, I don't have any spare change" or "I condemn you." Instead, he told her he was everything she was looking for in all her bad decisions.

This mess you've made of your life can be forgiven, and you can be changed. Jesus forgave that woman, and he told her to clean up her act and walk in faith. He'd done the same thing with another freewheeling woman who was about to have her head bashed in with rocks by a bunch of self-righteous hypocrites. Jesus stopped the mob by pointing out that the first stone should be thrown by the person without sin. They all slunk away, and he lifted that woman up. But he didn't just say, "You're forgiven, now be on your way." He said, "Go, and sin no more" (John 8:11 KJV).

Get up off the ground and change your life. Take this second chance and use it. This is not a get-out-of-jail-free card. It's a new beginning.

I'd talked to God quite a bit in my adult life, especially when I was high. Sometimes the Spirit would move me and the Lord and I would have good, long chats. Every now and again, God would talk back. I told you about the time back when I had some money and a house and a girl robbed me, making off with about four grand in amplifiers and equipment. Rage rose up in me. I wanted to find her, take back my things, and get a pound or two of flesh for the trouble. Instead of hitting the road in search of my stolen goods, I prayed for God to take the hot hatred away. That's when he came up in me and said, *Chill out, fella. It's only stuff. Material things mean nothing. They'll turn to dust, like everything else in this world. The Spirit lasts forever.* I'd heard him then. And I heard him a few other times, in jail cells and on cold nights outside.

The trouble was, I'd been asking for God's help but not listening to his full answer. He was telling me to forgive those who took advantage of me and be at peace with losing my things, but then he was saying, *Change your ways, so this don't happen again. Go, and sin no more.* For most of my life, I'd ignored that last part. I'd always figured that I could change my life tomorrow, or next week, or when the weather got warm, or after Christmas. There was always a reason to push the "sin no more" message down a rat hole.

Sitting against that fence, I was out of reasons. Out of push. I was out of time. I knew if I opened that bottle, I'd die in the street, a forgotten addict who'd squandered his talents and tossed away God's most sacred gift.

I put down the vodka and slid the bottle away so that it was just out of reach. Then I moved my legs underneath me, going from sitting to kneeling. I faced the sunlight so I could feel it on my face, even with my eyes closed. I clasped my hands together, something I hadn't done when I prayed since I was a kid. Then I spoke out loud, something else I didn't do much. A homeless man talking to himself sends people running, so I'd been careful to avoid getting verbal when nobody was around. This time it didn't matter. This was too important.

"Oh, Lord," I said, my voice quivering, "nobody deserves less from you than me. I've let things get away. I've wasted so much. I've thrown away so many of your gifts. I've done things so awful that I can't even say 'em out loud, even to you, knowing full well that you've seen it all. I'm a wreck, Lord. I'm the wretch that fellow wrote about in 'Amazing Grace,' so far gone that nobody'll look at me. I'm so sorry for what I've done, for who I've hurt, for the pain I've caused. I'm so sorry for the weakness. I'm sorry for the sins I've let build up like a pile of garbage. I'm so sorry for letting you down. I ain't wanting riches or success. I ain't asking for stuff. I just want to be close to you again. If you'll have me, Lord, I'd love to come back. Please, take this burden. Please, help me set things right. Show me the way. Not my way. Your way. Whatever time I've got left, let me live it for you. I want to be clean. I want to be forgiven. I want to walk with you, not on the other side of the road, but beside you. Even me, Lord. Even me."

———

It wasn't the longest prayer I'd ever prayed. It probably wasn't the best, since I didn't ask God to help others or to heal the suffering of my pals down the road. But it was the most real prayer I'd ever said. It came right from the gut, deep down, like I was pouring something out of my insides.

When I opened my eyes, nothing moved. No cars passed. Even I-40 was quiet. There was total silence. No bugs, no birds, not even a breeze through the leaves. A brown thrasher flew into the tree right above me, but other than that, the world as I could see it sat pretty still.

I stood up like a healed cripple. Nothing on the outside had changed. My shirt was still wrinkled and the knees of my blue jeans had worn down to the white. The teeth I'd lost were still missing, and I could've stood a hot bath and a haircut. Still, I felt clean, even though I needed to wash out my mouth. I felt strong, even though I probably couldn'ta run more than a block or two. I felt tall, even though I'd shrunk two inches from my height when I graduated high school. I felt full, even though I'd barely eaten enough to keep a squirrel alive. I felt secure, even though I was just as homeless and poor in that moment as I'd been for years. For the first time in over a decade, I felt truly and honestly free.

Ask anybody who's homeless, including me, what they see in it, and they'll all say freedom. There's freedom from bills, freedom from responsibility, freedom from the burdens of a life bound by someone else's rules. But that ain't real freedom. Like everything else in this world, that freedom can be taken away in a flash. The truly free find it on the inside, whether their body's living in a big house or a tiny jail cell.

———

I'd always heard Christians talk about being filled with the Holy Spirit. I figured that was church talk, words that signaled to others that you were in the club. That sort of talk couldn't mean anything real. How would being filled with a spirit work, exactly? Was it like *Ghostbusters*? Well, that morning in the dirty parking lot, I realized I'd been so wrong. Not only was the Holy Spirit real, but it did fill you up. I felt a warmness rinse me like a shower. Just then, the light reflecting off the church windows seemed to glow a little brighter.

There was a dumpster about fifty feet away on the other side of the church. I'd rummaged through there lots of times. I grabbed the vodka bottle, walked over, and tossed it in without so much as a second thought. It never occurred to me to keep it. The thirst was gone. I didn't want it, or need it.

Oh, there'd be temptations. Once the Devil knows where you live, he comes a-knocking. In the months to come, I'd need the help of others who'd been where I was. There were plenty of people to answer that call. I began working a twelve-step program, and I still take it one day at a time. But I'm comforted every day by what Paul, that fella who'd tried to smother Christianity in its crib before the Lord struck him blind on a dirt road, wrote to his friends in a town called Galatia. This one I know by heart: "So I say, walk by the Spirit, and you will not gratify the desires of the flesh. For the flesh desires what is contrary to the Spirit, and the Spirit what is contrary to the flesh" (Galations 5:16–17).

The flesh still tempts us. All of us. Every day. But I've walked that road. And I've walked in the Spirit. The Spirit is better.

———

———

Thirteen days after I found God and vowed to stay clean—it was a heck of a lot harder than just putting your mind to it—I got a call from my baby brother, Bobby. It was bad news. My stepfather had passed away. I cried, and I told Bobby how sorry I was that I hadn't been home with him. He was emotional, and not just about losing Dad. Bobby had handled everything—the funeral, the will, the house. He hadn't had time to grieve, so his feelings were raw.

"I've been sober two weeks," I said.

"Never heard that before," Bobby snapped back, which hurt, but he was right. At some point, I'd disappointed every person in my life, including my little brother. He wasn't about to accept my conversion based on the words of a homeless man.

"I know there's no reason to trust me," I said. "I hope you'll let me keep up with you. You'll see it's true."

"Yeah, well, that'd be nice, but I've got another problem," he said. "Dad left you some money. Five grand. I don't want to send it to you. You'll shoot it in your arm or smoke it or drink it. You might kill yourself with it. I don't know. But I know you'll blow it."

"Bobby, it's early, I know, but I'm changed," I said. "I can't explain how it happened, but God changed me. I'm a different man."

He laughed, but not like he'd heard a joke. It was salty. "Where'd you sleep last night?" he asked in a tone that said he wasn't expecting an answer. "God put you up at a Holiday Inn?"

———

That cut deep. Bobby had been my pride and joy, the baby I felt responsible for when I was in school. He was the brightest thing that happened to me after my dad walked out. It hurt to hear him be so cruel. True or not, we were brothers. I wanted him to share in my joy. But he was struggling. I understood that.

Then I said, "Bobby, I'm gonna give you an address." I gave him the street and zip code for the Little Pantry That Could. "If you want to send Dad's money, that's the place. If not, I understand." Then I said, "I love you, brother. I always have."

It got real quiet for a few seconds. Then Bobby said in a brittle voice, "I'll talk to you later," and hung up.

I'd love to say I didn't struggle after that. I'd love to say God made me strong, and I didn't have any temptation, but that would be a big lie. All the arguments I'd ever had with my stepfather, all the things I'd said intending to hurt him, flew back on me like buckshot. I couldn't remember the last time I'd spoken to Dad. Right after Mom died, near as I could figure. Did he know the struggles I'd had? Did he know the way I lived? Could he have imagined the drugs I'd taken, the liquor I'd drunk, the things I'd done to feed my addiction? I'm sure some family members had filled him in on the highlights. He had to have known that I was living on the street. Dad certainly knew that I hadn't made much effort to be close to him after Mom passed. Yet he'd left me five thousand dollars, a gift of love that he knew I could not repay.

Guilt and grief make a strong cocktail. After Bobby's call, I fought the temptation to drown my pain and sorrow in a brown-bag bottle with a handful of pills. That's when the Lord touched me again. I remembered another spot in the Bible, but it took me a little while to find it again. When I did, it was like James, the brother of Jesus and the fella who wasn't a disciple until he saw his own brother resurrected from the dead, was speaking right to me. "When tempted, no one should say, 'God is tempting me.' For God cannot be tempted by evil, nor does he tempt anyone; but each person is tempted when they are dragged away by their own evil desire and enticed" (James 1:13–14).

God doesn't tempt you. So when you feel temptation, you know it's coming from someplace other than heaven. Knowing that don't take the urges away. It just helps you tamp 'em down a little better. I'm addicted to drugs and alcohol, and will be every day I have left on this earth. I also got drunk and high because I liked it, a lot. I liked the way I felt when the dope kicked in. I liked the trips LSD took me on. I liked the way cocaine made me hear electricity running through the wires overhead and the whispers of people on the other side of the room. My devil didn't have horns and a tail. He came in a pipe and bottle, and I enjoyed his company, along with all the things that came with him. But recognizing the booze and the dope as the Devil helped me put them away. Whenever I saw a drink, or saw a joint, or knew that a line of cocaine was nearby, I imagined Satan standing there, red and ugly. That helped me put my desires away.

Before the week was out, a check for five thousand dollars showed up in Stacy's mailbox at the Little Pantry That Could. Because I didn't have an address other than the mission, and hadn't had a driver's license in more than ten years, I didn't have a bank account. The check-cashing place I'd used for my pay-checks and now, my Social Security checks, worried me some. I'd never had a check that big. I'd never held that much money in my hand. Ever. I was scared that I'd get knocked over the head and robbed, or that the cops would stop me and assume I'd held up a convenience store. Having a little money made me paranoid. Having that much made me a nervous wreck.

I didn't lose the cash or get mugged. Stacy kept most of it locked up for me until I could figure out what I planned to do. I'd need an ID and an address to open a bank account. It'd been a long time since I'd had either of those. There were some cheap apartments less than a mile from the bridges I'd slept under, a two-story place that looked like it might have been an old motel at some point. I walked there and put down a cash deposit. The apartment I got was on the second floor near the end of a long, concrete walk that each apartment door opened onto. It was all right. There was a bedroom and a small bathroom with a shower, sink, and toilet. Then there was a living area that opened to a small kitchen with another little area just big enough for a table and a couple of chairs. The floors had cream-colored carpet that was soft and warm on your feet. Most important, it wasn't in a drug neighborhood. Oh, it wasn't the high-end part of town. There was likely some illegality going on among my neighbors. But this wasn't a wide-open party spot. Cars didn't slow roll through the parking lot, stopping for a little commerce with a fidgety man on the corner. Women who looked half a day away from starvation didn't smoke outside while waiting on their next trick.

It might not have been the best place, but it sure wasn't the worst. I had a roof, a door that locked, walls, power, warm water, a stove for cooking, and a fridge for storing Cokes and leftover soup and beans. There was also a parking spot below with my apartment number painted on it. I didn't need that, at least not yet.

Between what I could dig out of dumpsters and what I could buy cheap at a local thrift store, I got enough furniture to move in. A bed wasn't important. That carpet was softer than the ground I'd been sleeping on and miles better than the concrete under the bridge. I found a couple of chairs in a dumpster, comfortable ones that fit just right in the living room. They were perfect for playing music and writing songs. A table at a salvage place cost me five bucks. I spent another four dollars for two kitchen chairs, which I could have made, but probably not for that kind of money. I bought a saw and some tools and made a standing table for the living room and a shelf. That shelf is where I put my tools, some duct tape, a can of WD-40, a hat, and a book or two, more stuff than I'd owned in more than a decade.

It worried me at first. Material things weighed you down. I felt dread at having to keep up with all that stuff. But then I sat down and thought about it, and I realized I was fretting over a roll of duct tape and a hand-me-down skill saw. If I kept my focus on the Spirit, I should be able to deal with a thing or two in my place. Jesus said, "Life does not consist in an abundance of possessions" (Luke 12:15). I knew that better than most. I also knew that worrying was like running in circles—it tuckered you out without getting you anywhere. Math had never been my strong suit, but I figured that, since I wasn't wasting money on booze and drugs, my Social Security check should cover the rent, power, and water. If I dipped into Dad's five thousand dollars every other month or so for food, I should be okay for a while.

Just like that, I was no longer homeless, although in spirit I still felt like I lived on the street. The friends I knew by name were the homeless people of West Nashville and those who helped them. I still had a longing to walk to the library and hang out during the day, even though I had a place of my own to sleep and stay warm. I didn't need to bathe in the creek anymore, but I still went down there. It was what I knew. Routine is hard to break. Even though I was a clean, sober citizen, saved by grace, I was, in my heart, a street person.

My soul sure felt better. God lifted the weight of being an addict off me. Even though the cravings came, I felt happy when I beat them. I felt like I could love people in the right way again, not because they partied with me or because I wanted them in an impure way, but because I could love them the way Jesus commanded us to love one another.

I thought about that prayer I'd lifted up in the Catholic church parking lot, the words I'd said out loud. Like everybody who'd spent more than a day or two in a Christian church, I knew the words to "Amazing Grace." What I'd forgotten was that the man who wrote it, John Newton, had been the captain of a slave ship. He'd found God in a storm off the coast of Ireland. I'd done awful things, but taking a ship to West

Africa, rounding up human beings, locking 'em in chains in the cargo hold, and selling 'em like cattle, well, I'm glad I didn't have those sins in my ledger. That first night in my new apartment, I picked up my guitar and played the hymn from memory. The words sunk in deep. *"How sweet the sound / that saved a wretch like me."* Even me, with all I'd done.

———

Reading became easy. It's amazing how clear your mind gets once you deprive it of chemicals. Memory was still suspect. Some of that stuff never comes back, but when the thickness in your mind finally turns loose, like sludge flushing through a broken dam, you see the world a lot better. Trips to the library got to be for books instead of makeshift beds. I could get the news on the Internet and sit in the chairs and read a magazine or a biography or a cookbook—anything I wanted. They even had music, which was great. I could listen to artists I'd never heard and pick out the songs I liked.

My trips to the Little Pantry That Could were more pleasant too. Everybody asked how I was doing. The hesitation in their voices told me that they were really asking if I'd fallen off the wagon yet. I understood that. A man's nature wins out most times. Suspicion softened after a while, though, especially once folks saw what I'd done with the money I got from Dad.

I still walked everywhere the bus didn't run. I'd carry my guitar downtown and play on the streets, propping the case open for tips. But I didn't count the money anymore. Before, I'd play till I got enough for crack, or smack, or whatever I needed that day. Nothing else mattered. Now I played as long as people wanted to listen. The money was an added blessing. I played some gospel songs in my street sets. I think people could feel how much they meant to me. *"Lord, build me a cabin in the corner of Gloryland . . ."* Songs like that always drew a crowd and some healthy donations.

I hadn't been in my apartment long when I was walking on the sidewalk past the McDonald's, and Stacy ran out and waved me down. "Doug, I've been looking for you," she said. "There are people in town from Sweden doing a documentary on street musicians in Nashville. I told them they had to see you. You have to play for them."

That was about as odd a greeting as I'd had in a lot of years. I think I said something like, "I don't speak Swedish." But Stacy explained that these folks spoke English, and it would be sub-titled when it aired over there.

"There's a woman who's a country music star in Sweden who has this documentary-type of show," she said.

"They have country music in Sweden?"

"I guess so," she said. "Anyway, this woman's got a film crew over here. They're wanting to show off the talent that's playing on the street. You'll be on television."

"Stacy, I don't want to do that," I said. "They don't want to see me."

"You're exactly what they want to see," Stacy said. "They're coming here. I need you to stay here so they can meet you."

"Okay, I'll do it for you," I said. I didn't have any plans. My

T-shirt was fairly clean, and I'd bathed. I didn't have my dentures, but that didn't keep me from singing. Playing for some strangers in the sunshine sounded like a nice way to spend a beautiful Southern day.

I milled around and spoke to several of my homeless friends. Stacy'd made coffee, and we talked about a few things going on in the neighborhood. I asked about some of the old crowd, but the answers I got were vague. That's the funny thing about being a recovering addict who's been saved by Christ. At first, you're scared of getting too close to your old running buddies for fear that they'll suck you back into the darkness. But after a while, once God takes ahold of you good, your old buddies get scared of being too close to you for fear that you'll suck 'em into the light.

After visiting for a spell, I went outside and sat on the ground, propping up against the church. Touching God's house always felt good, the cool stones against me reminding me of the sturdy Rock that had my back. I opened my case and put my standard sign in there, "Out of Work. Anything Helps," not expecting any cash out of this crowd. But you never knew.

Two cars pulled up slow. Even though we didn't have a driver's license among us, me and my friends all recognized 'em as rentals. Some instincts of street life never leave. Sizing up a vehicle and its occupants is a gut call that every homeless person makes. We know who's local and who's not, even if we've never seen them before. We know who's hostile, who's friendly, who's carrying cash, and, in most cases, we can guess how much. In this case, the two folks I saw get out first, a dark-haired woman in a hat and sunglasses and a taller man with short-cropped hair, not only weren't from Nashville, they weren't from anywhere I'd recognize. But I knew right off that they were musicians. I don't know how I could tell that. Maybe it was the muscles in their hands or the rhythm of their walks, but artists can spot other artists.

The woman was beautiful, with a big, inviting smile. Stacy came out and introduced everybody. The woman's name was Jill Johnson, and she said, "Glad to meet you," with about the cutest accent I'd ever heard.

I didn't know her, but Jill was one of Europe's bestselling artists. She was a country music singer and songwriter who'd brought old-soul country to a place where that kind of music was new. Her good looks and charm made her a big hit in Sweden, and television producers had bugged her for years about putting on some sort of reality show. She didn't want to do a variety show or a singing contest like the ones in America. None of the other reality shows she'd seen looked like much. But, as she was building a front porch on her house (something they don't have a lot of in Sweden, I found out later), an idea struck her. She thought she'd travel to different places in America, particularly the South, and find interesting musical stories. That show would be called *Jill's Veranda*, named after the porch.

Turns out, she'd been doing it for a while with a lot of success. With cameramen and a couple of sound people following her like pups, Jill had toured the American South, hitting up churches and picnics and finding folks who played music on their own porch swings. She'd played and sung for inmates in a Tennessee prison, and she'd followed fellow Swede Adam Baptiste to a music festival where they'd jammed with some great bluegrass artists. She'd even been to Emmylou Harris's house and sung a song or two with Emmylou. I didn't know about that when I met Jill or I'da been too jumbled up inside to speak, much less sing.

Gram Parsons had been dead forty years—morphine and booze, a combo I'm sure I'd tried a time or two, although it was hard to remember—but his songs with Emmylou still rattled me. For Emmylou to take to Jill told me all I needed to know about the country music siren of Sweden. In another of her shows, Jill had sung a duet of the Stevie Nicks song "Landslide" with Veronica Maggio. I didn't know about that until much later, either, but once I saw it, I had to wait a minute or two before talking.

This time she'd come to Nashville with the tall fella, a man named Magnus Carlson, a great musician and songwriter who had a band in Sweden called the Weeping Willows. They set out to find street musicians. Magnus could have been a salesman at Guitar Center, for all I knew. Seemed like a nice man—a little hard to understand, at least at first—but I still didn't get what they hoped to find on this trip. Stacy'd said I was exactly what they were looking for, but I didn't know what that meant.

A few minutes in and their motive didn't matter. If I'd been wearing socks, Jill woulda charmed 'em right off me. A buddy of mine named John, who lived in his truck, sat down and enjoyed a cigarette next to me, and Stacy sidled up close. Another homeless friend named Kim Netherton came and hung out with us too. Jill's smile was like a magnet, but not in a way I woulda thought a few years before. I saw a light of goodness in these people—something the stoned me wouldn't have seen.

I told 'em I'd been in Nashville for fifteen years, and most of that time I'd been homeless. I told 'em about the shelter and the bridge. It always stuns people. Most professionals have never had a conversation with somebody who's been homeless. They don't know how to react. Do you apologize? Do you say, "Oh, that's interesting"? When a fella says, "I've slept under a bridge and eaten out of a dumpster," what's the next line in the conversation? Jill and Magnus didn't know. They fumbled around for a second or two before steering the discussion back to music.

My friend Kim told them, "I love country music. I like Johnny Cash. He had some rough times too. He got labeled. I think the ones that are homeless, we get labeled. 'They're homeless. Don't talk to 'em. Don't touch 'em.' We're human. We have feelings. And we don't bite."

Her face tightened, and nobody could speak for a few seconds until Magnus moved in and gave her a huge hug. They both had to take a minute after that.

I gave Jill and Magnus a brief history of my life in music: Grandma, Mom, Dad, and my move to Nashville from New York. I left out the bad stuff. That wasn't for strangers. I didn't say much about it to my friends either. Many of 'em were still struggling with drugs. I didn't push. There's nothing that'll put you off quicker than a newly sober addict telling you all about it. I figured they'd see the changes in me soon enough. Love shown in silence makes an awful racket in a sinful man.

Jesus told us not to point out the splinter in your brother's eye when you've got a stick of lumber in your own. Working with wood my whole life, I understood that better'n most. But the Lord didn't stop there. Most folks, when they're throwing that line out, end it right there, because they're telling a friend or family member to shut up, to look after theirownselves and not worry about the sins you're doing. Jesus also said, take out that plank in your own eye so that you can see. Then help your brother get that splinter out of his own (Matthew 7:5).

I had a lumberyard in both my eyes. But I was getting 'em out, one by one. Friends saw it. Even if words on the matter never passed between us.

Once the camera and sound guys were ready, Jill and Magnus squatted down to be eye level with me. Then I launched into "Going Down to the River."

> *I'm going down to the river*
> *to wash my soul again*
> *I've been runnin' with the Devil*
> *and I know that he's not my friend*
> *I've been falling by the wayside*
> *living in this world of sin*
> *I'm going down to the river*
> *gonna wash my soul again.*
> *I'm going down to the country*
> *to bury my head in the creek*
> *I'm gonna jump in those waters*
> *and baptize both my feet*

'Cause everywhere I been runnin'
  I been getting in trouble deep
I'm going down to the river
  gonna wash my soul again.
Well, this ol' world's going to hell
  in a handbasket
If I don't get me some restoration soon,
  I'm gonna end up in a casket.

Magnus had this curious look on his face. I could tell something was puzzling him. It was like he couldn't believe he was hearing this out of a toothless guy he'd met outside a food pantry for homeless people. Jill hummed along and nodded. I think she liked my voice, but she seemed curious about the song too. When I finished playing, they stood up and clapped, which was nice.

Jill said, "Wow, that was amazing. What song is that? Is that your song?"

"That's my song," I said.

"That's your song?" Magnus said, and he looked at Jill as if he didn't believe it. Then he said, "That's better than all the songs we've ever made."

That embarrassed me, which was not how I normally handled praise. But these weren't fans on the street. These were pros, people who had hit records—people who knew the business. Maybe it was Magnus's words or the fact that I'd been so blessed by God already, but I felt overwhelmed by these folks.

"That's incredible feedback," I said. "That's worth a lot more than money to me."

Magnus stood still. He kinda looked lost. Then he said, "That's the most beautiful thing that I've heard in . . . I don't know when."

"Oh, come on," I said, putting my hands up and dropping my head. These people didn't need to say that. Telling me "good job" or "that's real nice," was one thing, but them going on with this sort of praise was almost too much. The thing I knew right away, though, was their words were genuine.

"The words . . . they . . . they go straight to the brain and to the heart," Magnus said. "Just amazing. Wow."

Jill jumped in and said, "That song should be recorded."

I couldn't let the opportunity pass without letting them know who I was now. I said, "You know, God gave us music. God gave us the human voice, the greatest instrument in the world. People who think they can't sing are highly mistaken. Because music is therapy. That's what it's meant to be. That's how you feel it."

I played a couple of more songs, a slight up-tempo version of the "Boll Weevil Blues": "*Well my name is Mr. Weevil, but my best friends call me Boll . . . I gotta go, baby.*"

Once the cameras were off, Jill and Magnus hung around a little longer and listened to more stories from the families at the Little Pantry That Could. In three years, Stacy'd gone from feeding fifteen families to having about a hundred and forty come in every Saturday for food. I could tell the stories touched Magnus deep down. His entire demeanor changed. Music was why he'd come to Nashville, but it was obvious that he was leaving with a whole lot more. The people and the stories had moved him. This wasn't a television show for him anymore. It was a mission.

The show's producer, a young woman named Agnes Akerlind, suggested that we all ride downtown so we could shoot a little introduction for this segment of the show. I wasn't sure how all that worked, but I had nowhere to go, so we rode off together to Third Avenue, to a corner near a hotdog stand where I normally played. There was a metal bench with an ad for Grumpy's Bail Bonds plastered on the side. I'd seen that ad plenty of times, usually outside holding cells at various precincts. I'd never used Grumpy's. When I got arrested, I never had enough money to pay a bondsman, so I sat in jail until trial, no matter how small the charge. Today I was outside enjoying the sunshine and singing like a bird. I played a couple of up-tempo boogie-woogie songs first and then a few ballads before covering some old-time Charley Patton stuff: *"I gotta move to Alabama, to make Georgia be your home."*

Agnes set up this fiction where they filmed me playing on the bench and had Jill and Magnus wander up as if they were finding me for the first time. Agnes also went over and talked to the guy who ran the hotdog stand—I'd known his name at one point, but that part of my brain had long since short-circuited— and he said he'd love to be a part of it.

"I've told everybody that comes by here that they ought to listen to Doug," he said. "Might as well do it on camera."

So the camera guys set up and shot Jill and Magnus as they got hotdogs with onions and relish. Then they filmed me playing a blues song as the two of them walked up like we'd never seen one another before. I explained my homelessness to them for the cameras again and suggested that we go out to the Little Pantry That Could, even though that's where we'd originally met. My acting wasn't the best, I'm sure, but everybody said it made for a great introduction to the television show.

That was it. After a little more visiting, everybody said good-bye and we all went our ways. I didn't think anything more about it. I hung out with my friends downtown a little while. Then I went back to my neighborhood where I saw a couple more friends before heading back to my apartment. Another day without a drink. Another success. That and prayer were all that mattered.

I didn't know what Magnus and Jill were doing. I'd barely thought about them since our time together the day before, although I did wonder if I'd be able to find Jill's TV show on the Internet. Turns out, while I was drinking coffee with my buddies after the crew loaded up and went on their way, Magnus made a big decision during his car ride with Jill. The original plan for the show had been for them to head over to Memphis where Magnus would record "Always on My Mind" in Sam Phillips's famous Sun Studio. That'd be the big highlight of the show. But Magnus told Jill and Agnes that he wanted them to take me into the studio. He wanted "Going Down to the River" to be recorded.

Things got quiet and he got a lot of nervous looks. It was one thing to video a hobo sitting on the ground outside a food pantry. It was something else to rent studio time for him. What if he froze? What if he had mental problems and had a spell in there? What if he made a bunch of outrageous demands after production? What if this, that, or the other thing? Magnus stayed firm. His day at the Little Pantry That Could had changed him. He wanted to shine an even brighter light on the humanity that lives in the shadows. He felt called to showcase the talent living in those who get ignored. The best way to do all that was to get me recorded. That way the people of Sweden, and hopefully people around the world, would have a constant reminder of the less fortunate. Every time they saw a rerun of Jill's show, every time they hummed that song, they'd think about that guy on the street asking for a handout. Hopefully, they'd have a little more compassion and understanding of the folks they went out of their way to avoid.

Agnes had to scramble. The Memphis part of the trip was canceled and somebody got aholda John Carter Cash. He invited 'em to the Cash Cabin, the studio at Johnny Cash and June Carter's old home place. But there was another problem. Nobody had any idea where I was or how to find me. I hadn't gone by Stacy's place. I wasn't at the Nashville Rescue Mission. I hadn't told anybody where I was going or what I was doing. I was where I always was: around.

Stacy, the camera people, Jill, Magnus, and Agnes drove around Nashville looking for me. They'd stop on the corners and under bridges and ask other homeless people if they'd seen me. They flagged down cops and asked if anybody knew where I was. After an hour or more of searching—just about the time they were ready to give up—one of the production guys drove past a corner and saw me playing.

I didn't know about any of this until they all showed up.

At first, I thought I mighta done something wrong. Why was everybody out looking for me?

Then Agnes said, "We'd like to record 'Going Down to the River' with you at the Johnny Cash Cabin. Would you do that?"

"I don't think the bus runs out there," I said.

"We'll drive you," she said.

"Well, that's very kind of you," I said. "It's overwhelming, really."

Magnus chimed in and said, "No, Doug, you are overwhelming."

So we rode out to Hendersonville to the Cash place where Jill had a sound engineer and some studio musicians ready to go. I got chills walking into the cabin. This was where Johnny had cut all his later work, including all the Grammy-award-winning stuff with producer Rick Rubin. I'd never been close to this property, but I knew the names of the people who'd worked in the same rooms I stood in that afternoon, people who'd stood on those same floors. Everybody from Vince Gil to the Nitty Gritty Dirt Band had cut songs in this cabin. John Prine, Kris Kristofferson, Elvis Costello, Tanya Tucker, T Bone Burnett, Chet Atkins, Waylon's boy, Shooter Jennings, who put a good edge to his old-style country sound—even the late Chris Cornell of Sound Garden and Audioslave had ventured out here in the woods to cut a record. It felt like a dream that I was about to do the same.

I don't know how Jill, Magnus, or Agnes charted the music to "Going Down to the River" so quick, but those studio boys knew what they were doing. The only thing I was unhappy about was the drummer sitting behind a full kit. "Going Down to the River" didn't need drums, but I didn't want to be rude, especially since I was a guest. So I asked the guy, "Have you ever seen one of those boxes that guys sit on and play?"

He said, "Oh, you mean a cajon."

I said, "That's it. Would you happen to have one of those in your car?"

He said he didn't. "All I've got are some bongos," he said.

I said, "Perfect. Would you mind getting those?"

He left, and we started recording. I felt bad about it. After I got a little experience, I realized that those guys are professionals. They understand when you don't want a particular sound. I tricked a guy to pull him off a drum kit when all I needed to say was, "Hey, this song doesn't lend itself to that much percussion."

Then I gave some instructions to the guitar player, which prompted another round of strange looks from Jill and Magnus.

"How do you know about recording?" Jill said.

I told her about the EP I'd cut at Monster Studios. Then I said, "I used to play with Buddy Miller."

I'm not sure if any of 'em believed me, although I hope I didn't look like the kind of guy who would lie to your face. After everybody got set up, we went through the song one time with the three of us. I sang the first verse, and me and Jill harmonized the chorus. Jill sang the second verse, and we went to a bridge where the guitar player did some cool improvisation. Then Magnus reprised the first verse and we harmonized the chorus again. After we played it back, I thought it sounded great, better than I could have imagined. I'd played that song so often, out loud and in my head, that I knew what I wanted it to sound like if it ever got recorded. Now that it had, I was right pleased.

I figured we were done, but everybody insisted that I cut a solo version. So we went through another couple of takes—no more than two—with just me singing. Magnus and Jill couldn't have been more complimentary. They went on and on about how much they loved my sound, my music, and my story, and how proud and moved they were to have met me. That praise was even more overwhelming the second time around, but I figured that they weren't really seeing me; they were seeing God through me.

Either the producer or Jill, I can't remember which, told me that the version of "Going Down to the River" that the three of us laid down would close out that episode of *Jill's Veranda*. It was a beautiful mixture of Jill's mellow tones, Magnus's rich tenor, and me, so I figured it'd be good on TV. I just hoped I looked all right for the camera. I wasn't as polished as Jill and Magnus, but they seemed happy, so I was too.

They drove me back to my apartment and we left, promising to keep in touch, although I felt certain I'd never see any of them again.

That turned out to be wrong in a big way.

My life went back to normal after that. I played on the street every day and went to meetings for addicts. I talked to friends and made a few new ones. Coffee and conversation with the recovering working girls at the Thistle Stop Café and Reverend Becca, the owner, replaced afternoons in crack dens. I still went to the library and read and enjoyed meeting as many new people through music as I could.

Not quite three weeks after my visit with the Swedes, I was walking to the library. Just before I got there, a guy on the sidewalk stopped, pointed, and said, "Hey, you're Doug Seegers, aren't you?"

I said, "Yeah, how'd you know that?" My first instinct was that I was in trouble for something, that this was an undercover cop who'd been looking for me for some crime I didn't remember committing.

The man said, "You've got the number one song on iTunes in Sweden."

"Get outta here," I said.

"No, I figured you knew," he said, and shook my hand. "Congratulations."

I stood stone still for a second, not sure what to do. Was this guy kidding? I didn't know there was a Swedish iTunes. So I went to the library and got onto a computer. With a little help from a patient librarian, I surfed around until I found the Swedish version of iTunes. I didn't know any Scandinavian, but I didn't need a translator for what I saw.

"Going Down to the River" by Doug Seegers was a number one hit.

———

Eddie Stubbs, the voice of the Grand Ole Opry, asked me on his radio show not long ago, "Doug, what took you so long to make it?"

I said, "I wasn't thinking about making it. I was thinking about living."

———

That's partly right. I think that every person has a time and a place and a purpose. But it's all on God's time, not ours. People think in terms of their own plans, not God's. They say, "God, why did you take my job away?" "Why did you take my house away?" "Why did you take my parent, or my spouse, or my child?" Then they get frustrated by the silence. And that's when the Devil pops up, saying, *Things aren't working out for you, so God's not real. Give up.* Or even worse, *This is all God's fault. Blame him.* But God doesn't work like we do. He works in millions or even billions of years. It's impossible for humans to understand his timing. If you're upset because he didn't answer your prayer from last Thursday, you need to look at yourself, not him.

He waited sixty-three years to use me. Now, I'm not going to waste another day.

There's this part in the Bible about looking at the birds in the air, about how beautiful God's clothed 'em. And how they're fed every day, even though they've never planted a single crop or stored a single grain. If God will do that for a bird, what'll he do for us? (Matthew 6:26).

I know the answer. He'll make you an example at exactly the right time, not that fits your plan, but the time that fits his.

Look at me.

CHAPTER 8

CINDERELLA MAN

Sitting in that library, I wasn't sure what to do. Seeing my name on the computer screen, not as part of a police report, but as the singer and songwriter of a number one hit record, well, that sent all kinds of emotions running through me. My breathing got quick and I felt my face tingle. I hadn't expected the song we'd recorded in the Cash Cabin to end up on iTunes. I didn't even know when Jill Johnson's show aired. I stared at the screen for a good, long while, and I must have hooted or chuckled, because the librarian who'd helped me patted me on the back. I think she congratulated me, but I was so numb, I don't remember thanking her. It didn't seem real. Then I asked myself: *What does this mean?*

Confetti hadn't fallen on my head. Nobody'd shown up at

my door with balloons and an oversized check. I wasn't sure what happened when you had a hit record. People had bought my song, obviously, but where'd that money gone? I didn't have a record contract. It was my song—I'd written it and recorded it with the help of Jill and her television team—but I didn't know the first thing about the business side of selling music, especially not in the iTunes era. The vinyl records I grew up with were what college kids bought to be retro. Other than a few side-street shops near campuses and coffeehouses, there weren't any record stores anymore. Music was different now. How it all worked was a mystery to me.

The tears surprised me. I'd tamped down my dreams for so long that when they came true, I let loose a flood. I didn't know I had all that pent up. They were tears of joy, but also fear. These were waters I'd never tread. I felt sure my life was about to go in a different direction. I just wasn't sure how. Even when you know a change is good, it still makes you tight. An hour before, I'd walked into that library as a street musician living on Social Security and tips—a saved sinner fighting the Devil every day to stay sober and sane. I walked out as a bestselling artist. Where I went from that point, I had no idea.

I headed back to my neighborhood and told everybody. Stacy and Becca got emotional with me. They didn't know any more specifics about what having a chart-topping song meant than I did, but they agreed that my life was about to be much different. We talked about Sweden, and why my music and story might strike a nerve over there. Later, I went back to my apartment and prayed. I thanked God for blessing me like this, but I also prayed for strength. Temptation would be calling soon enough. I didn't know much of anything about the modern music industry, but I was sure of that. People would be watching me to see how I handled these gifts. It was time, after all these years, for me to set an example.

I still worry that my story will send the wrong message. Giving myself over to God the way I did, and then having such life-changing success shortly afterward, I fret that folks might say, "Money's a little tight in my house. Maybe I should ask Jesus for a raise." That's not how it works. God's not a Lotto ticket. Finding him, no matter what your circumstances, does not put you on a glide path to prosperity.

John the Baptist, the world's first evangelical, was beaten, tortured, thrown in a hole, and finally got his head lopped off for preaching the truth. His belief didn't make him rich or successful. Peter, the man Jesus built his church on, had done all right for himself as a commercial fisherman before dropping everything to follow Christ. How'd that work out for him? The Roman emperor Nero, who burned Christians at the stake to light his dinner parties, crucified Peter upside down. James, the brother of Jesus (and this is how you know the Gospels are true: What would it take for your brother to convince you that he was the Son of God?) was also executed for spreading the message of Christ. These were Jesus' most devout followers, the folks who'd walked with him, who'd seen the miracles, who'd written down the things he said, who'd seen him dead, buried, and risen, and they were, almost to a man, put to death. The only exception was John, who lived in exile in a cave. Not exactly a life of luxury.

Turning your life over to God don't mean you'll get a number one song, or sell your first novel, or get that promotion. There's a bunch of suffering Christians all over the world who'd think you'd lost your mind if you preached 'em that message. Throughout history, Christians have taken the opposite route I did. They had plenty of material things until they turned their lives over to Christ, and then they suffered awful. From Roman emperors killing 'em for sport to terrorists blowing up their churches on Easter, Christians have paid a heavy price for their faith from the get-go.

Having a bestselling song happened because of God. But if I'd been struck blind on the street and had my voice taken away, that, too, would have been from God. My job was to praise him either way, to use the gifts he'd given me to spread his message. Peter, the disciple Christ said would build the church, said, "Yet if any man suffers as a Christian, let him not be ashamed; but let him glorify God on this behalf" (1 Peter 4:16 KJV).

Suffering or success, your job is the same: let the world see Christ through you. The blessings God gave to me were part of a plan much bigger than one hit song. He made the decision that I was going to be a living testimony. Once he makes that call, you're obliged to do it right.

It took me some time to figure out exactly how to do that.

What didn't take hardly any time was my phone ringing. A hit record brings 'em out quick. Just a day or two after being stopped on the street and told I had a chart-topping single, my cell phone rang, which was peculiar. Very few people had my number. I answered and heard a thick accent. The fella said his name was Bjorn Pettersson and that he was from a management agency in Sweden called Rootsy Music. I found out later that Jill's management company, Lionheart, had called him and told him about me.

"I have experience in both Nashville and Sweden," he said. "I'd like to talk to you about cutting a record and see what kind of interest you have in coming over here and touring."

My first question was how this stranger had gotten my number, but I had so many other questions that I let little ones like that slide. I'd been living in Nashville for fifteen years without so much as a sniff of recognition in the music industry, and out of the blue, I had a fella from the other side of the world calling me about going into the studio.

"Okay," I said. "Who are you?"

For the better part of two and a half hours, Bjorn gave me a brief history of his life and why he was so interested in me. He was a musician and a promoter who put together tours for artists all over Europe, but primarily in Sweden where he lived. He'd also worked in the prison system in Sweden for twenty-five years, rebuilding broken lives and turning men away from a life of crime. In addition to all that, he'd been a foster parent for four children, bringing them into his home and raising them to be responsible people in the real world.

In just about every way imaginable, Bjorn had seen broken people with busted lives, boys who'd been tossed out like yesterday's newspaper and men who'd let this demon or that ruin them in ways they regretted every day. His calling was to help all of them, to provide inspiration and hope where none existed.

So when Jill's show aired, her management company reached out to him and asked him if he'd like to help.

At first he wasn't sure he wanted to be involved. That was one of the reasons for this phone call. If this was a sideshow—bring the helpless, homeless man to Sweden and tour him around like a trained monkey—Bjorn wanted no part of it. He was feeling me out as much as he was telling me about hisownself. Like the producer of Jill's show, he needed to know that I wasn't one of those poor street souls who fight the voices in their heads. He also wanted to hear about my homelessness.

I told him, sparing nothing. The drugs, the booze, the loneliness, the despair at not making it in music after coming down to Nashville, the women, the sins, and the salvation—he needed to know it all.

We talked about his love of country music and how Sweden had embraced authentic country artists. "That's what you are," he said. "Authentic." He also told me that if I was just looking for a quick buck, there were ways to cut a record, book some shows, get in and out fast, and be on my way, but he wasn't the guy for that. But if I was looking for a more long-term career path in music, he could help develop the lasting relationships to make that happen.

The only thing I'd ever wanted was to make it in music. Money had never been the goal, because I'd never had any. I asked Bjorn how this would work, and he said he had a relationship in Nashville with a producer named Will Kimbrough. That stopped me cold. Everybody in country music knew Will Kimbrough. He'd written songs for Jimmy Buffett, Little Feat, Todd Snider, and

Jack Ingram and had worked with Emmylou Harris, Rodney Crowell, John Prine, the Jayhawks, and Roseanne Cash, among many others. He also was such a great guitarist that he'd won the American Music Association Instrumentalist of the Year award in 2004, dethroning none other than Dobro maestro Jerry Douglas. Surely this Swedish fella wasn't about to put me in the studio with Will Kimbrough.

I tried to contain myself, but when I asked if he meant *that* Will Kimbrough, and Bjorn said he did, I think I hooted into the phone.

"We have a lot of work to do," Bjorn said. "I need you to pick out songs. Come up with a list, and I will call you and listen to what you've picked out. Do you have access to a computer?"

The library was my only computer access, but I knew that I could get help from Stacy and others. We agreed to talk again the next day, and the day after that, working out all the details of how we'd pick out songs and talk through them together.

In the meantime, "Going Down to the River" became number one on Spotify. According to Bjorn, you couldn't walk down the street in Sweden without hearing it on the radio or coming out of the speakers at stores or restaurants. I closed my eyes and tried to imagine that. When I was a kid, my dream had been to have my songs on the radio. I'd listen to Cousin Brucie on WABC play the Byrds and imagine that the next words out of his mouth were, "And now, we've discovered this new cat with a happening sound. Here is . . . Doug Seegers." Those dreams weren't just vivid; they were a place, a spot I could go to whenever I needed to comfort myself. I didn't know what the

Swedish equivalent to Cousin Brucie was, but the reality of having a radio hit was different than my dreams, but better in one important way: When I was a kid, I wanted the fame and glory for myself. Now I wanted to use whatever fame I got to spread God's Word through my story.

More film people showed up, a different bunch this time. Jill's show had aired just a few days before, and another team of documentarians—a word I'd only heard in passing and had sure 'nough never used—came over from Sweden wanting to make an entire show, an hour-long documentary on my life. They wanted to call it *Cinderella Man: Doug Seegers*. They said they wanted to follow us during the making of the new record and whatever kind of tour Bjorn set up afterward. I didn't have any glass slippers, but I did have an unseen force guiding my life. If they made God part of the story, I didn't mind showing 'em around.

New people were flying into my life so fast I didn't know how to react, so I upped my praying quite a bit. When you're homeless, you get used to being in a certain circle of folks. Strangers pass through but only to the extent that they're serving you food, or listening to you play on the street, or arresting you. Having all these people introducing themselves and heaping all this praise on me . . . I'm sure glad I wasn't a younger man who didn't know the rat hole you can fall into if you let praise go to your head.

I took the film folks down to the culvert where I lived for a while and to the woods near the creek where I bathed. I showed them the mission and the street corners where I hung out and played for tips. As we were going through the highlights of my story—and I was newly sober enough that I didn't share it all—I told them about hanging out with prostitutes and I used the term *partying* to describe boozing and drugging like a man with a death wish.

"You know, these girls who live out on the street, getting high, they're throwaway children," I said to the producer. "That's what I was. I was a throwaway child. So I related to 'em."

Old men cry a lot. I didn't hold back during that filming. As I've stayed sober and made praying part of my daily routine, my emotions have evened out, but I'm still moved to tears a good bit. I just don't cry for the man I was anymore. That was part of God's plan. You can't be sad or upset when you're on the road he's laid out for you.

I took those documentary boys to the Little Pantry That Could. Stacy gathered a big group together for a mini concert. A buddy of mine named Lloyd, who I met sleeping under the bridge about four years before, offered to play with me. We'd played a lot together on the concrete at night before falling asleep or passing out. I'd just written "Angie's Song," which I'd hoped would be the follow-up single to "Going Down to the River." It took a couple of minutes for Lloyd to find the rhythm and chords, but he made a good backup player that afternoon for a house full of folks.

Stacy told the cameramen, "Doug makes this music from his heart. If you've heard it, you know that. He just wants to make people happy." That summed it up better than anything I ever wrote.

———

For three weeks, Bjorn and I talked every day. I played the songs for him, communicated all the lyrics and the licks and talked about the details of each one. I didn't know what he was doing behind the scenes, but as I prayed for guidance, God told me that this was a man I could trust, a man whose goal was to help me, not to use me.

Bjorn had called Will Kimbrough while the famous producer was on the road, driving down Interstate 65 from Nashville to Mobile, Alabama, where his parents lived. That's about a five-and-a-half-hour trip, so Bjorn had plenty of time to fill him in on my story. Will took to what Bjorn told him, especially when Bjorn compared my sound to Gram Parsons. That's one of the best compliments anybody could have paid me. Having my name mentioned in the same breath with one of my musical heroes was a bigger deal than anybody knew. Bjorn also sent Will a clip from *Jill's Veranda* and a computer link to the Cash Cabin recording of "Going Down to the River."

Will liked the sound. He called Bjorn back and agreed to work with us. The problem was timing. This was March. The record had to be out in May so I could start touring in Sweden. That compressed timing worked out to be the best thing that could have happened to me. Will, needing to put a band together quick, called his buddies, a group he had been playing with for several years. They were called the Red Dirt Boys, and they were Emmylou Harris's band. It was an avalanche of riches, and every day I had to both thank God and pray for strength not to let any of this puff me up. The mission was the message. All this other stuff, as cool as it seemed, was just the train to get there.

———

Three weeks later, me and Bjorn met face-to-face. He'd brought along another fella from Rootsy Music named Hakan Olsson, and the two of them showed up at my apartment looking like lost sheep. I got the sense that even though they'd been to Nashville before, neither of them had been to this side of town. Few in the music business stopped south of Charlotte Avenue. Once they were there, though, we hit it off real good, and a relationship began that would grow into true brotherly love.

———

Will set everything up at Sound Emporium, the studio where everybody from B. J. Thomas and John Denver to Taylor Swift and Robert Plant had cut records. The soundtracks to the movies *O Brother, Where Art Thou?* and *Walk the Line* were made there, and photographs of Patty Griffin, Elvis Costello, Willie Nelson, and Kenny Chesney lined the walls. Not only had I never been in the building, I'd never been to that side of town. Once you become homeless, your world shrinks. My West Nashville neighborhood and the area around the library and mission, that was my area. Sound Emporium was only six miles southeast of my apartment. On a warm day I could have walked there. But it might as well have been on Mars. Now, I was there with a producer, an engineer, and a studio full of professional musicians. I brought a guitar and a composition notebook—the kind kids take to school—full of my songs.

We had three days to cut the record.

After shaking hands with Will, the next person I met was

a redheaded woman named Barbara Lamb. She wasn't part of the Red Dirt Boys, but Bjorn had brought her in because she was such a great fiddle player. I liked her immediately, and she would become a big part of my story. Todd Robbins was my engineer, another stranger I was meeting for the first time, but a guy I learned later had a great reputation in town.

Then I met Phil Madeira, who played guitar, accordion, keyboards, lap steel, and just about anything else we threw at him.

"Interesting story," Phil said. "My daughter knows you. When I got the link to YouTube [to the *Jill's Veranda* piece], Will said, 'Hey, check this guy out, you're going to be playing with him in a week. My daughter Maddie, who busks downtown, said, 'That's Doug.' So I said, 'You know Doug?' She said, 'Yeah, I know Doug. Everybody knows Doug.'"

That was far from true, but we hoped more people would know me by the end of that summer than knew me that second in early April.

Will and I worked through the songs. I don't know who'd charted them, but everybody seemed to know the music when I got there. It was so amazing to hear my songs performed so professionally. Some of those songs on the record were twenty years old and a couple I'd only written two weeks before. This was a chance for all of them to shine.

The last thing I wanted was to tell these pros how to do their jobs, but nobody knew these songs the way I did. If something wasn't right, I had to let 'em know in the kindest possible way. Honesty in all things would be my top priority, part of my new life in the Lord. As long as I accounted for my reasons, and did it without sounding brash, those guys would get it, or so I hoped.

They must have sensed my unease, because the drummer, whose name was Bryan, came up to me after the first run-through and said, "Doug, if there's anything you don't like, just let me know. I can change anything you want."

I said, "Bryan, I don't know a lot about drumming, but I know when I hear something that's not right, so I'll let you know."

That broke the ice. The rest of the session, those guys and I worked through several songs. We rerecorded "Going Down to the River" and a love song called "Memory Lane":

> *Lord, there's nothing more precious*
> *Than these memories from you*
> *All the good times, the bad times*
> *Hard times we made it through*
> *You were my guardian angel*
> *My addiction from hell*
> *But only Jesus really knows*
> *All the love that I felt.*

Hearing my song played back with accompaniment—mandolin trills, a steel guitar, soft snare with brushes, a lonesome fiddle's cry—it brought me to tears again. I'd sung those lyrics on the street more times than I could count, but having a song like "Memory Lane" produced by Will and played by these pros made it brand-new.

It took a few tries to get "Angie's Song" perfect.

———

Let me be the one who finally takes down that
pusher man
When you finally lose your appetite.
Let me be the one who walks to the liquor store
With someone else tonight.
Let me be the one who gets down on his hands
and knees
And thanks God that you're all right.
Gonna be all right, baby.

I'd written those words deep in the cellar of heartbreak and addiction. When Angela first left me, I drank and cried for a solid two weeks before writing the first of three songs about her. As we laid down the vocals for "Angie's Song," they took on deeper meaning. I wondered how many people had gotten down on their knees and prayed for my recovery, how many friends had worried that I might not make it through any given night. Sometimes it's hard to imagine others having the same worries for you that you're having for other people. You're concerned that the people you love are killing themselves without seeing the knife you're holding to your own throat. It doesn't take long for sober eyes to see the scars in your reflection. The truth was, I had plenty of angels who wanted to take down the dealers who kept me high; plenty of friends who learned how to forgive because they didn't want to lose their road to glory; plenty of loved ones who would've let me cry on their shoulders, if only I'd been conscious enough to see 'em.

After a good session, Will said, "I've got a surprise for you."

I asked for a hint, but he wouldn't give up anything. Good thing I didn't know what was coming. I'd already gotten emotional. Breaking down again would have been way too much.

———

Buddy Miller had gotten an e-mail from Will saying, "I'm working on an interesting project with this street musician who's been homeless. His name is Doug Seegers. I'd like for you to sing with him on one of the tracks."

Well, Buddy didn't know me as Doug. He'd met me as Duke and had always called me Duke, so he didn't make the connection and didn't get back to Will right away. So Will called Buddy as he was in his car driving north out of Nashville.

"Hey, Buddy, I've got that guy I e-mailed you about in Studio A," Will said. "He's got a real different sound, a great story. He says you know him."

Buddy was busy and wasn't paying much attention, so he said, "I'm sure he's great, but I don't think I know any Seegers."

Will said, "You knew him as Duke the Drifter."

Buddy hit the brakes and turned the car around. Just like that we were reunited for the first time in forty years. I finally got to apologize for the way I'd left him all those years before.

Buddy's wife, Julie, a bestselling recording artist and Texas girl who I knew back when she was Julie Griffin, came to the studio with him. It was a grand reunion for us. They'd been living in Nashville almost the entire time I'd been there, but I never attempted to reach 'em, not at my best and certainly not at my worst. I guess I figured those days, those relationships, were behind me.

Buddy brought in a picture of the two of us playing the Back Room in Austin back in 1976. We looked like kids. I could barely speak to him, because it was so overwhelming to have him reappear in my life after all that time. We did our best to pick up where we'd left off—the good parts, not the parts where I disappointed him—but when we hugged, it was like another weight fell away.

"Did you hear 'Going Down to the River'?" I asked.

"It flipped me out," he said.

"Buddy, I didn't know the song was that good," I said. And I really didn't. It was certainly heartfelt. I'd written it at a time when the words had been more of a cry to God than something I thought about selling or even singing for very long. My spirit needed cleansing when I put those words in my notebook. That's probably why the song touched so many people. I'm not the only one who needed to wash my soul again.

Buddy and I played and sang together on a swing tune called "There'll Be No Teardrops Tonight." It was like we were back in Texas, singing duets every night to a crowd of beer-swilling cowboys and buckle-bunny honeys (Texas slang for girls who hang out at honky-tonks in tight jeans with belt buckles the size of dinner plates).

I'll pretend, I'm free from sorrow
Make believe that wrong is right
Your wedding day will be tomorrow

But there'll be no teardrops tonight.
Shame, oh, shame for what you're doing
Other arms will hold you tight
You don't care, whose life you're ruining
But there'll be no teardrops tonight.

It was a grand old time. We told stories about those days in New York and our road trips through Texas. Laughter danced through that studio like no time had passed at all, even though everyone knew the paths our lives had taken. You couldn'ta found two people further apart in terms of what we'd done. Yet there we were, Buddy and me, old friends who'd spent fifteen years living ten miles from one another, but who might as well have been in different worlds, reunited, bonded by music and a kinship that never faded.

"It's probably a good thing you didn't make it in the business earlier," Buddy told me. "It would have swallowed you up."

"We wouldn't be sitting here if I had," I said. "Graveyard's full of musicians like me. I'da been right there with 'em."

Then I thought for a second and said, "Everything has a season and a purpose under heaven."

"Ecclesiastes," Buddy said.

"Borrowed by Pete Seeger and the Byrds," I answered. Everybody got a kick out of that.

We worked in the studio for three days. That record ended up with twelve songs, a good number of them ballads, along with a few honky-tonk tunes that would fill a dance floor. The most offbeat track was another song about Angela called "Burning·

———

a Hole in My Pocket." Will wanted to add horns to give it a boogie-woogie feel. I wasn't sure at first, but once I heard it, I was glad I didn't put up a fuss.

> *The way you do the things you do*
> *eating my heart out with your eyes*
> *The way you make me feel so young*
> *walking around mesmerized*
> *You lit a torch in my soul*
> *like a shiny bottle rocket*
> *Oh, Angie, my sweet thing*
> *burning a hole in my pocket*

Will had a few more surprises. On the song "She," he asked Emmylou Harris if she'd sing backup after we finished. That floored me. Since my days following the Flying Burrito Brothers, I'd loved Emmylou. Her duets with Gram Parsons were still some of the most soulful in all of country music. The idea of having her featured on my record was beyond anything I'd ever dreamed.

After the third day, Will played the whole thing back for me. Once again I had to take a minute. Like I said, old men cry more than we should.

CHAPTER 9

"EN AV VÅRA EGNA"

The success in Sweden baffled me, and it continues to leave me shaking my head. The album came out in May and shot up the charts. "Going Down to the River" stayed at number one for two weeks and hovered in the top five pretty steady for many months after that.

Bjorn and Hakan helped me with all the paperwork that goes with publishing, and Barbara Lamb, who'd played fiddle on the record, and who went by Babs, jumped in to help with my day-to-day management. For years, my day-to-day needs consisted of eating, sleeping, and getting high. Now I had to have somebody field a hundred phone calls, handle interview requests, coordinate release dates in different time zones, and work through legal documents that might as well have been written in ancient Greek. Again, it would have been easy to slip, to backslide into a drink or two. The Devil puts that thought in the addict's head every day. As you get deeper into recovery, ignoring him becomes easier. But he never goes away.

During those early days, one of the main things that drove me to stay away from my old ways was the support of my friends. I could have gone back under the bridge at any moment. But my angels—Stacy and Becca and Brian Irwin at Monster Studios, who took me off the street and recorded an EP for me at no charge—they were so proud of me. I didn't want to let them down. Then there were the folks who still lived on the edges, my buddies John and Lloyd and so many others. Women who still sold themselves. The throwaways. They were watching. They were pulling for me. They were, hopefully, seeing themselves— seeing what was possible, seeing theirownselves through me. I couldn't disappoint them. I couldn't kill their hope.

Babs made a few phone calls and got me in touch with a local lawyer who could review documents and help me through some minefields. Jack Roscoe, the man who'd fired me for punching a coworker in his woodshop and rehired me because the love of God lives in him, helped me set up bank accounts and explained, as much as he could, wire transactions. He also asked his pastor to haul me down to the DMV to get a new driver's license. It'd been a dozen years since I'd lawfully operated a motor vehicle. Getting back on the road worried me, but Jack said I didn't have to drive if I wasn't ready. Having the license would allow me to get into federal buildings wearing something other than handcuffs, get on an airplane, check into a hotel—things I was going to need in the coming weeks.

The line at the DMV stretched halfway around the room, but Jack's pastor knew somebody and got us moved up. After filling out a few forms and passing a vision test, I was legal to drive again and had my first government-issued picture ID in years.

Even after he went back to Sweden, Bjorn kept in touch daily, not just because of the business, but because of his genuine desire to see me succeed in life. Like my other friends, I think he feared that I'd fall off and be back under the bridge at any moment. That didn't hurt my feelings. Having people fret about you is humbling. It was even more incentive for me to stay on the straight and narrow. I'd always been the guy who cut off his own nose to spite his face. You think I ought to behave a certain way, I'd show you by doing the exact opposite, even if it landed me in jail, which it did more than once.

Bjorn also worried because a man's mind don't kick into high gear right away when you've been high for most of your life. My short-term memory loss and trouble concentrating frustrated me once I realized that I had it. Bjorn would have to repeat things three and four times because I'd forget 'em from one hour to the next. Babs got impatient at times, and I understood it. Mix ADHD with four decades of drug abuse and you get a fella who misses more than a few details and has trouble holding his thoughts. A lot of people never come back from the injuries they inflict on their brains with drugs. I'm thankful that, in time, I could organize my thoughts and memories a lot better. In the beginning, that was not the case.

———

During one of the calls right after the album was cut, Bjorn said, "I've got seventy tour dates scheduled, and they're all sold out."

"Did you say seventy?" I asked. "Seven zero?"

"Yes, that's right," he said. I guess he assumed I couldn't understand his accented English, but I just couldn't believe my own ears. Other than a few club gigs in a bygone time, I'd barely played in front of seventy people. My head got light thinking about standing in front of one packed venue after another.

There were some problems. For starters, I didn't really know where Sweden was. If I had a map of Europe in front of me, I could wave my hand over Scandinavia, but that was as close as I got. And I knew nothing about the language or culture. Jill Johnson, Magnus Carlson, Agnes, Bjorn, Hakan, and the folks who had come over from the television crews were the only Swedes I'd ever met in my life. What kind of food did they eat? What side of the road did they drive on? How many of 'em spoke English? Was there coffee over there? These questions seem silly now, but at the time they had me worried. I'd never been out of the country, and outside of Spanish Harlem and pockets of Texas, had never been anywhere that the predominant language wasn't my own. The idea of heading to this place for an entire summer, maybe longer, made me tight.

One problem from my past almost derailed the whole thing. My Tennessee driver's license got me into the government building to apply for a passport, but it didn't clean up the mess I'd made in years gone by. A young lady behind a Plexiglas window handed me the paperwork to get a passport, which I filled out on the spot. I handed her my ID, the forms, those mug-shot-looking pictures you get, and a cashier's check for the processing fee. Minutes later, she came back and said, "I'm sorry, there's a hold."

"What does that mean?" I asked.

"There's a hold," she said again, as if the same words a second time would clear the whole thing up.

"What's a hold?" I said. "I don't know what that is."

"There's a legal hold," she answered in a slightly irritated voice. "You've got some outstanding legal issue. You can't get a passport till it's cleared up."

"I'm supposed to leave for Sweden," I said. "I've got seventy shows booked."

If she cared, she did a great job hiding it. Without so much as a "just a second," she walked back to her desk and hit a couple of buttons on her computer. Then she gathered my ID, photos, and forms, handed them over, and said, "It's from State of New York Child Services."

I'd left my wife when my son, Jacob, was one. I'd left New York when he was thirteen (although in my drug-fueled mind, I thought he was fifteen). That meant I had several years of child support due to Lynn. Once I fell into addiction and homelessness, those debts built up. Another dark stain on my history, another failure, another sin. I called the lawyer that Babs knew and explained my predicament.

"The ticket's bought, and the dates are booked," I said. "I've gotta get there. My whole career could be over before it starts."

The lawyer reached out to New York Child Services, and

to Bjorn, and to the State Department. Nobody at any level of government seemed anxious or understanding. They'd do what they did at their own pace. The attitude was, if I'd paid the support in a timely manner, I wouldn't be in this predicament. My lawyer explaining that I'd been living under a bridge at the time didn't seem to sway any feelings. So I could do nothing but worry as the lawyer sent money to New York, back payments, plus interest, plus court costs and penalties. Then we waited while the paperwork was slow-walked through the system. I'd dealt with the courts enough to know that nothing happens fast, which had me in a near panic.

The day before my flight, I was convinced that I wasn't going to make it. Bjorn was surprisingly calm. He'd booked venues, sold tickets, put up deposits, had a media and marketing plan, and now everything was in jeopardy because I hadn't paid my obligations on time.

My flight left Nashville for JFK at 3:00 p.m. on a Tuesday. My passport came through at 11:00 that morning.

I'd never been on a plane before and never been through airport security. Thankfully I didn't take a pocketknife. Jerry Miller was a guitar player in Nashville who Bjorn hired as part of the band. He and Babs were my unofficial minders, making sure I got to the airport with my tickets and got on the right plane. Babs picked me up at the apartment and we met Jerry at the terminal. Luggage wasn't a problem. The only thing I had was a guitar in a case, the clothes on my back (a T-shirt from La Zona Rosa, a cool music club in Austin that I'd gotten at Stacy's pantry), two T-shirts, and a toothbrush in a bag.

"That's all you have?" Babs had asked as she drove me to the airport.

"Yeah," I said. "Should be all I'll need."

"You're going to be gone for almost four months."

"I've lived with less than this for fifteen years," I said.

Babs just shook her head and mumbled, "Four months."

If you've flown your whole life, you don't think anything about it, but when you experience takeoff for the first time in your midsixties, well, I was pretty drawn up. About an hour in, we hit a patch of turbulence. I said a quick prayer, then looked at Jerry sitting next to me, who was reading, not at all concerned.

"Jerry, I'm a little worried here," I said. "Would it be all right if I held your hand?"

"No," he said, pulling away from me.

Laughter calmed me down. When I'd get a little antsy again, I'd reach over for Jerry's hand. He'd swat me and slide as far away as possible.

———

Bjorn kept my arrival in Sweden a secret. 'Course, my first question was: "Secret from who?" Who on earth would care that some old American was making his first trip to Stockholm? A businessman from New York wearing a nice suit sat next to me on the flight from JFK, and we visited a good bit. He asked why I was going to Sweden and seemed interested when I told him my story, but other than that, I didn't expect anybody to give two hoots about my travels.

———

I couldn't have been more wrong.

Bjorn was waiting at the gate for me when we landed.

"Is that all you brought?" he asked, looking at my T-shirt bag and guitar, which got broken during the flight.

"What else do I need?" I asked.

There was a long pause. Then he said, "The Red Cross is on the way. We'll stop and pick up a few things."

Bjorn also told me that we needed to be quick and quiet getting out of the airport. The press had been after him like bloodhounds. Word had spread about all the shows he'd booked for me, so everybody wanted to interview me and get me on television. I didn't care one way or the other, but Bjorn said, "You're not ready. We're not ready. I want you to get acclimated to where you are and what's about to happen."

Since I'd never been on a jet, I didn't know what jet lag was, but I was bushed and coulda stood a nap. On our way to the Red Cross we stopped at a fast-food place and I got a beef and bean bowl. Because I'd been flying so long, I took out my dentures and put them on a napkin. 'Course, one of us threw them away. We were already in the car and on our way when I realized I didn't have my teeth. So we went back and rummaged through the dumpster to find them.

I could see from Bjorn's face that he was thinking, *What have I gotten myself into?*

So I said, "Hey, this is nothing. At least we're not looking for dinner in here."

We found my teeth, bought a few more T-shirts and a couple of pairs of jeans at the Red Cross, and then Bjorn took me to the hotel. I'd never stayed anywhere like my room in Stockholm. Everything about it made me feel out of place. Of course, I was exhausted by the end of the first day. I couldn't wait to get to sleep, but the bed was too nice for me to lie in. I would have felt terrible messing up those beautiful sheets. So I took a blanket and extra pillow out of the closet and slept on the floor, a surface where I felt right at home. I'd expected to wake up back in my apartment in Nashville, or maybe on the cot in the mission, or in a box under the bridge. It had to be a dream. The next morning the hotel was still there, with bottled water in the nightstand, a coffee pot next to the television, and the softest, thickest towels I'd ever seen.

A friend was there too. That first full day, Magnus Carlson came to visit. He hugged me and asked me how I was doing. We visited a good long time.

"Doug, I couldn't be happier for you," Magnus said. "If I can do anything to help—"

"You've done more than enough already," I said. "If it wasn't for you, and Jill, and the good Lord, I wouldn't be here."

"You deserve every bit of it," he said. "I know you'll be great."

For the next week or so, Bjorn quietly showed me around Stockholm and the surrounding countryside. It was a beautiful place that reminded me of upstate New York with rolling fields and old hardwoods. The city was clean and the people were friendly. Bjorn was right: it took a few days for my head to clear. I had to get acclimated to the air, the time zone, the food, and hearing a different language spoken all day every day. It was different. Swedes walk different in their own country than they do in America. Turns out everybody drinks coffee from tiny cups that they keep on a tray in their kitchens. And you'll get invited in for a cup by nearly everybody you meet. You gotta be careful or you'll be so wigged out on caffeine that you won't be able to sleep.

It took nearly a week before I could lay in the bed. Turns out, when I'm adjusting to something new, old habits creep back. Lying on a hard surface was so ingrained in me that I couldn't fall asleep any other way, especially with all the excitement going on around me.

I didn't realize it at the time, but Bjorn was easing me into the life of a professional musician. He was also feeling me out to make sure I wasn't going to fall off the edge once the tour got going. Jesus was tempted. To figure we humans won't be is foolish. I don't blame Bjorn one bit for keeping a close eye on me in those early days in Sweden. If I'd been in his shoes, I would have done the same. Even before I'd left Nashville, after *Jill's Veranda* aired, Swedish people who lived in Tennessee would stop me and say, "Are you Doug Seegers?" sort of gushing like I would have if I'd bumped into Paul McCartney on the street. I can't lie; that attention boosted me up and made me feel special. I had to pray for strength to keep those feelings in check.

Bjorn also put the band together. Except for Jerry Miller on guitar and Babs, who came over later and played fiddle with us, I had an entirely Swedish band, a group of solid pros who knew the scene and understood what to expect. They were the band for a Swedish folk singer named Ellen Sundberg. At the time, my brain was still in the process of healing, so I had a hard time remembering their names, but they didn't mind. These weren't partying kids. They were mature musicians who understood what was at stake. If I messed up, it'd be big news in Sweden and a sad story back home.

So we slipped out to a little yellow house near the highway. Back home it could have been one of those places where I'd spent the night with a lost woman, popping Xanax and whiskey. Now it was a place where beautiful music came together. Ellen sang backup and the band jelled quick. Me and Bjorn couldn't have been happier.

I still hadn't made any public appearances. But as I felt more myself in Sweden and Bjorn got comfortable with me, he reached out to a friend for my coming-out party.

Magnus and his band, the Weeping Willows, had a show at a place called the Cirkus, an arena-style venue that seats 1,650 people and looks like the king's summer palace. He invited me to come out toward the end of the show and play "Going Down to the River" with him. By then, a Swedish woman living in North Carolina had made me a couple of suits, dark ones with swirls embroidered on the shoulders. I also got a dark cowboy hat and a white bandana. Backstage at that Cirkus (which was built in the 1800s for a permanent circus in Stockholm), I was a nervous wreck. The largest crowd I'd ever played for was two hundred people, and that'd been forty years ago with Buddy. The crowds in Nashville who'd hung around to hear me on amateur nights topped out at about thirty, and most of them were there to drink. Playing in front of a crowd that size, my heart jumped pretty hard.

Bjorn was there, and he told me to take some deep breaths, which I did. I also closed my eyes and prayed, out loud, but soft and slow. I prayed for peace and strength, and for the hope that at least some of these people would somehow be led to God by my story. Calm came on me. I didn't tighten up or shake at all. My voice was just right. I heard Magnus say something in Swedish, and then "Doug Seegers," which was my cue to walk out.

I'm old enough to remember when the Beatles came to New York. The screaming and hollering and cheering. It was like nothing anybody'd ever seen. I can't say this was just like that, but it's the closest I've ever seen since then. All 1,650 people in that auditorium erupted in cheers that went on and on, not slowing down or quieting down, even after we started playing. If anything, the noise got louder once I started singing. I'd always heard about crowds being "electric," but I never knew what that meant. I'd had some nights when I felt revved up by folks cheering. But this was something bigger. I could barely hear myself and couldn't hear Magnus, who was standing two feet away. When the song ended, the cheering got even louder, which I didn't think was possible.

That's when I realized that this gift I'd been given was bigger than I could have imagined.

———

The first show was June 9 in a town called Skebobruk, which would be a suburb of Stockholm if Sweden had suburbs. By that time, Bjorn was the most hated man in Sweden, at least by the media. He'd turned down a solid two hundred interview requests. There'd been one day when I sat for interviews with about a dozen journalists. Most of 'em wanted me to repeat my story about being homeless and how Jill had discovered me outside the Little Pantry That Could. They wanted to know what I thought of Sweden, but at that point I hadn't seen much outside of Stockholm and the house where I rehearsed with the band. I wasn't sure how I'd done in those interviews, but Bjorn assured me that I'd been perfect, giving them exactly what they needed. After that day, Bjorn shut the media out. No more interviews. They carried on and called him names, but he insisted that I was touring and could not be rattled. That set 'em off even more. Stories ran about Doug Seegers sightings. People who'd sold me a cup of coffee, or seen me on the street were interviewed, like I was Bigfoot or something.

I didn't understand the marketing side, and I didn't question what Bjorn was doing. Turned out to be the right thing, though, because the people couldn't wait to see me when I finally got out on the road.

Most of the venues were going to be small, just like this first one in Skebobruk, where we would play five nights in a row, but I was still jumpy as a yearling deer.

"Don't worry about being nervous," Ellen said before we went out onstage. "I'm there and will help you with the lyrics when I'm singing backup if you forget."

"That's good, because I am nervous, and when I get nervous I forget things," I said.

The words to songs usually came to me. When I put the

guitar in front of me, it was like I became a different man, because that's when God spoke through me. Without it, I was just Doug, the guy who couldn't remember your name two minutes after I met you. In the middle of a song, the Spirit of a higher power used me, and I did all right.

When I heard my name, followed by some Swedish words I didn't recognize, I took off my hat, squeezed my eyes shut, and said, "Thank you, Jesus." Then I walked out onstage for the first time with my own band in more than twenty years, and for the first time in my life as a chart-topping artist.

The reaction was not what I expected. These people cheered and clapped and jumped up and down, and cheered some more. It was like Beatlemania except with an older crowd. I hugged Bjorn after that first show, probably a few seconds longer than I should have, but I was just so grateful to everyone, it was overwhelming. The second and third days I signed autographs, posed for pictures, and sold copies of the CD. One woman told me she hadn't felt that way since the time she'd met Rod Stewart. I'd been compared to a lot of folks in my life, but that was a first.

By the end of June, I felt like I had my footing. I played in Umeå, a beautiful college town in the north on the Ume River that has one of the most magnificent churches I've ever seen, with spires that look like they're reaching all the way to heaven. I didn't have time that trip to see much of the city, though. The next night we were in Piteå, a midsized port town on the northernmost edge of the Baltic Sea. Then we were back in Stockholm at an amphitheater. The crowd went wild at that one. It's like I was Justin Bieber for the over-fifty crowd. Right after that, we played an outdoor festival in a place called Kiruna, the northernmost town in all of Sweden about ninety miles inside the Arctic Circle. I figured it'd be snowing in June up there, but it was a beautiful city—an old iron-mining place where reindeer roamed around—and the weather was perfect. I don't know how many people were at that show, but I couldn't see the back row from the stage.

Places I couldn't pronounce—Uppsala, Trollhättan, Högmarsö, Sundsvall—we played from the southern tip of Sweden to the northernmost outpost. Sometimes we rode the train, but Bjorn also hired a car and driver to get me from one spot to the next. As I slept on the road, my mind drifted back to the Chevy van Buddy had in Texas. Tip to toe in Sweden didn't come close to driving from El Paso to Texarkana. And the trains were a lot more comfortable.

In the category of "Things I never thought I'd learn": When you're onstage and a big crowd starts swaying in front of you, you better focus on one or two people down front or you'll get seasick. You also need to find a routine on the road or you'll be worn out in a week.

Travel beats on you, but I wasn't about to complain. This was what I'd dreamed about since I was a child. Sweden was never part of my plan. Even as a kid, I'm not sure I knew anything about the country, which is a shame given how the Swedes embraced me as "one of their own"—*"En av våra egna."*

I rode from the far northeast down to Halmstad, another college town on the west coast where we played another outdoor show for a group of people who loved to dance like I'd never seen. Swedes doing the Texas two-step is a sight to behold. Then I celebrated the Fourth of July on Väddö Island in the Baltic, the other side of the country.

One routine that kept me grounded was busking on the streets during the day. I'd always been a street performer. From my hippie days playing for tips in New York to my homeless days in Nashville, going to a street corner and striking up a tune always turned me on. It was even better in Sweden because it was so unexpected. We were selling out shows every night, so nobody expected to walk down to the corner and find me and Jerry riffing some old-time country and blues. Some folks didn't think I should do it. Jill Johnson, who continued to be a great supporter, said, "Doug, you play music for a living now. People pay to hear you. You shouldn't give it away on the street." But that's like telling a fish not to swim. Meeting people on the street, seeing the expressions on their faces, watching them nod and move to the rhythms—that's why I did it. It was in my blood. I'll never quit it. If I'm breathing, I'll be a street artist.

I'll also never forget the hard times, and the feeling that hope was for other people. Right after one of our shows in Stockholm, I asked Bjorn about his work in the prison system. Several people during our tour had come up to me before and after shows and said things like, "Your song 'Going Down to the River' saved my life." That was powerful, and humbling. I'd written that song about needing to cleanse myself of my addictions, needing to ask God to wash away my sins, needing to go down to the creek and wash the inside, not just the outside of myownself. But as I told Buddy Miller when we were recording the record, I didn't think the song was that good. Obviously, God used that song, and me, in ways I didn't expect.

If my words were touching people in life-changing ways, then I needed to share my story with the most downtrodden among 'em. Jesus didn't hang out with the rich and famous. He had dinner with Zacchaeus, the most hated man in town, and he told a hardened criminal, "Today you will be with me in paradise" (Luke 23:43). The least I could do was go play for some guys who couldn't come see me in person—not because they didn't want to, but because they were behind bars.

Jail in Sweden is different. The folks inside spend their time preparing for a productive life on the outside. They study and develop usable skills, go to counseling and therapy, all with the goal of reintroducing themselves into society with positive results. The punishment isn't the prison itself. It's being deprived of your freedom. I understood that better than anyone. Some of the jails I'd been in America, where jails are rotten, were still warmer than the bridge. The beds were cleaner and more comfortable than cardboard and concrete, and the meals easier to find. But you weren't free. You did what you were told, when you were told.

Bjorn did a lot of work rehabilitating prisoners, helping lost souls get their lives back on track. So after a show in Stockholm, I asked him if we could make a visit to some guys who were behind bars, to see if we couldn't shed a little light into their lives and brighten at least one of their days. We rode up to Anstalten Norrtälje, the Norrtälje prison, where I could play for the men who were where I'd been—men who were struggling to find their way.

They were sunning in the yard when we got there, the barbed wire glistening in the summer rays. "Angie's Song" was first. I told 'em, "My girlfriend spent time in jail. She was a drug addict and an alcoholic. I wrote this when I got sad about her sitting in jail. It was therapy for me. That's why I wrote this song."

When I sang "Going Down to the River" for them, those young men lit up like kids. They were, at least for that moment, happy.

Everybody falls. And everybody can be redeemed. That was my message to those men in that prison. It's the message I try to spread every day.

———

Seeing those young men, and hopefully touching their lives in some small way, laid a need on my heart. My son, Jacob, was about their age. It'd been seven years since I'd seen him. I'd never get that time back, but I could at least reconnect with him now that I had my life together. He knew that his father was a homeless addict. I wanted him to receive the same message that I was trying to spread through Sweden, and really, everywhere people saw my story or heard my music. I wanted Jacob to see that turnarounds are possible for everybody. Even those you've given up on.

He wasn't sure about coming. It's not like we were asking

him to drive down to New Jersey. Dropping everything to spend
a few weeks in Sweden took some work. But, after a little plead-
ing, Jacob said he'd come, so Bjorn set up the trip. Nobody told
me my T-shirt was on inside out when I went to pick him up at
the airport. He was sitting by a coffee kiosk when I saw him.
My gracious, how big he'd gotten. He was a full-grown man
and more handsome than I'd ever been on my best day.

We hugged, and I let another tear or two slip out. I took
him to the hotel and got him settled in, and then we went to a
car show in a park north of Stockholm where I was playing a
gig. I felt like I'd been thrown back in time to when my uncle
had taken me and Dave to see the muscle cars on display at the
beach. There was a classic Bonaventure convertible, a pristine
GTO, a 1957 Buick Century with whitewalls so bright they
hurt your eyes. Jacob got to see me play a few songs solo on
a small stage beside the car show, the first time he'd ever seen
me play for an audience—first time he'd ever heard claps and
whistles for his father.

I don't know what he felt. I hope it wasn't what I'd felt for
my father after he walked out on us. But I couldn't blame him
if he resented me or even hated me. I'd earned it. Too often a
man becomes the thing he despises most. I'd become a drifter
musician, a honky-tonk ladies' man, a drunk. I'd become my
father. That yoke weighed heavy. I just hoped it wasn't too late
to mend the wounds that I'd caused in my own son.

Jacob sold CDs and T-shirts during the tour. He didn't
believe me when I'd told him how big and crazy everything had
gotten. Like me, he didn't know anything about Sweden, so

wrapping his arms around an old man singing roots music over there and being treated like Justin Timberlake or somebody—that didn't compute for him, just as it didn't register with me when I first arrived.

Our time together wasn't easy. We talked and struggled and hugged and cried. I hoped he didn't think I'd brought him over to show off. I wanted him to see what I was doing. Not because I wanted to say, "Look, your old man's a big shot." I wanted him to see that his dad was sober, clean, and saved. I wanted him to see what a difference God made. I wanted him to witness the miracle and to take the message home.

But before he went, I wanted Jacob to meet my newest guardian angels. In August, I finally reunited with both Jill and Magnus at the Stockholm Music and Arts Festival, a giant summer party on the island of Skeppsholmen. Because of our schedules, I hadn't seen Jill face-to-face since our time in Nashville. We'd talked. She'd kept up. But I certainly hadn't had the chance to thank her good and proper for everything she'd done for me. Because of her, I was wearing new boots, playing a new guitar, headlining sold-out shows, and falling in love with a new country. She had saved my life. She'd launched my career at an age when most musicians have long ago hung it up. The two of them, Jill and Magnus, were angels of life and light, whether they saw it or not.

I got together with Jill at the sound check early in the afternoon before our show. She was stunning as ever and hugged me a good few seconds. That was important for Jacob to see. He needed to witness his father being spiritually connected with people without anything bad involved. He'd never met Stacy Downey, who I still call the Mother Teresa of West Nashville, but my son got to meet Magnus Carlson and Jill Johnson, the people who started this whirlwind of a story.

That night, as the three of us played and sang "Going Down to the River" in front of tens of thousands of people, I was struck by how quick God works when he's ready. You can spend decades of your life lost in more sin than most humans can imagine. But when the Lord's ready to use you, he don't dally.

"A city set on a hill cannot be hidden. Nor do people light a lamp and put it under a basket, but on a stand, and it gives light to all in the house. In the same way, let your light shine before others, so that they may see your good works and give glory to your Father who is in heaven" (Matthew 5:14–16 ESV).

CHAPTER 10

BEAUTIFUL BOY

I t's easy to pray when you're hungry—easy to fall on your knees, face the sky, and ask God to show mercy on your sinful self when you haven't had a meal in a day and a half, when night's coming, the ground's hard, the wind's cold, and you don't know how you're gonna sleep with an ache in the pit of your gut. It's easy to pray when you're lonely—easy to call on the Lord to heal a broken heart and take the blow of rejection away, easy to ask him to pull off some magic and bring a happy ending to a hurting time. It's easy to pray when you're out on the street, when the world seems against you, when you can't seem to get up before being knocked down again.

Turning to God in sorrowful times—in grief, turmoil, poverty, or the self-inflicted messes of life—that's just easy; it's expected. Almost everybody who's down and out will eventually put their hands together and ask God to throw 'em a line. In that old movie *It's a Wonderful Life*, George Bailey's sitting at a bar when he says, "Dear Father in heaven, I'm not a praying man, but, if you're up there and you can hear me, show me the way. I'm at the end of my rope." That happens so often that we're surprised when it don't.

What's hard is continuing to pray once the world gets good to you. There's this old joke about a woman who's on her way to have an affair with a married man when she runs her car into a ditch in a rainstorm. The water's rising, and the woman thinks she's gonna drown, so she prays to God to help her, swearing she'll change her ways, dump the boyfriend, and do volunteer work at a battered women's shelter if the Lord'll just save her. Right then, a man in a truck sees her, stops, hooks a cable to her car, and pulls her to safety. The woman then speeds toward the meet-up with the married guy. She says to God, "Never mind. This fella in a truck got me out."

Like that woman, I was in a ditch of my own making, only worse. I'd dug every inch of mine. I'd abused my body and addled my brain in ways that probably should have killed me. I'd fought with family, said the most hurtful things to people I should have been loving, given up on my marriage, invited the Devil inside every time he came knocking, and, yet, if you asked me now, "Doug, how'd you end up under a bridge, having let so much of your life slip by?" the answer would be three words: drugs and alcohol.

Most of our sins can be whittled down to a word or two,

maybe a sentence, but no more than that. All the pain you felt when you found out your spouse was cheating, all that trouble you went through, all those tears you cried, all the anger and fear, and the legal crap you had to go through, the new apartment you had to find, the friends you lost, the looks you got; all those times you lashed out at people who didn't deserve it, burdened people with troubles they didn't need to hear, all that grief you slowly worked through; years later, when you're asked to tell your story, you probably say, "I went through a rough divorce." That's it.

I saw it in jail so many times I lost count. "Why're you in?" You don't get the life history of a boy whose father beat his mother and left them with nothing; you don't hear about the longing a boy has for an older man to look up to, the hunger he has for somebody to tell him how to do things, how to shave, what to wear, how to talk to people on the street, and how to be a man. You don't hear about the ache he had for some structure and some belonging, no matter how sideways it seemed from the outside. You don't hear about the initiations and how it felt to be accepted. You don't hear what his mother said when she learned what he was doing. You don't know what he felt when he picked up that first gun. All you know is the answer he gives. "Armed robbery."

The girls who come through the Thistle Stop Café in West Nashville could fill you with stories that'd leave your jaw hanging open. Most of them were abused early. Most by family. All of them ran away from something or someone. They tried to fill the holes in their hearts the only way they knew how: by letting guys use 'em, abuse 'em, pay 'em a few bucks for their bodies, and do awful, degrading things to 'em. They did those things to eat, and maybe find a bed at night. Those who get out—the ones Becca Stevens rescues and resettles in a new life—won't talk about it. Their one sentence is, "I did bad things in a bad place."

It's easy for me to let my story sit where people see it. I was a homeless drug addict who got clean, found God, got discovered by playing a song for a Swedish documentary crew, and became a bestselling artist in a new land. But that wouldn't be right, because, while true, it's not the whole story.

Temptation came to me, not in the way I thought it would—drugs and alcohol—but where I least expected it: fame and fortune. I'd always thought it'd be easy for me to go back under the bridge if I had to, to return to the streets and enjoy the freedom I'd had as a homeless person if my career went south. It wasn't about the money, and I didn't care about the fame, I told myself.

Then the Devil dragged me up on a high mountain and showed me the riches of the world and said, "All this can be yours." Well, that's not exactly what happened. My temptation came in a series of phone calls from lawyers and producers and promoters back in America saying, "We can make you the next Garth Brooks. We want you to come home and be a star. We want you to hit the real big time. All you have to do is dump that bunch you're running with over in Sweden."

Jesus faced temptation and said, "Get behind me, Satan!" (Matthew 16:23).

I said, "Let me think about it."

Bjorn had become like a brother to me, so I needed to talk to him about what these guys were saying. I didn't realize at the time that he was catching flak from all sides. Not only were some guys in the States trying to undercut him and get me to come back home, lawyers from the record label were yelling at him, telling him that he had no contractual rights to book shows for me, but they also threatened to sue him if he even talked to me. That was silly, especially since me and Bjorn traveled together that entire summer and had meetings every day. But that was how crazy things had gotten.

Not knowing anything about the music business, or any business for that matter, was a great thing because the entire experience was like a wide-eyed kid going to Disney World. That's part of what drew so many people to my story. The downside was, business can be dirty. And any time there's money on the line, people will line up to get some, whether or not they have your best interests at heart.

Bjorn had been managing me from the moment he contacted Will Kimbrough about putting together the first record, but he told me up front, "I'm not a manager. I'm a promoter. I book tours and put on shows. I'll manage you during this first tour, but we will need to find someone to take that part of your life over after the summer."

I didn't know what a manager did, but I knew that I couldn't book my own hotel rooms or manage the money that was coming and going. I could order and pay for coffee, but that was about it. Anything more complicated than that, and I needed some assistance. Part of it was the fact that my brain hadn't yet healed the way it would in the coming months, but I'd never had a business of my own either. At my peak, I was lucky if I stayed employed at the same place for more than a couple of years. None of the moving parts of operating a business made any sense to me. I didn't even know where the cash went from the records we sold after the shows. I just played, sang, signed autographs, posed for pictures, thanked everybody, said a good-night prayer, rode to the next show, and started all over again.

Babs Lamb was somebody I trusted. She'd played a mean fiddle on the first record and seemed to take a maternal interest in me. We connected right off. So when the time came for some-body to be my official manager, I said, "Why not Babs?" Bjorn wasn't sure how that would work, but Babs seemed smart and organized, so he wished her well and turned over the day-to-day stuff to her. He had his hands full with American lawyers and other Swedish musicians.

When I wasn't on the road, Bjorn did put me up at the house where the Rootsy Music offices operated. There was a room in the back near the kitchen, and it became "Doug's room." Our daily meetings would take place at the kitchen table where Bjorn and Babs would go over everything we were doing and needed to do in the next twenty-four hours. I remembered about 10 percent of what they said. And by the next meeting I'd forgotten that. All I really understood was that the record had gone plati-num and continued to sell, and we needed a follow-up record and tour. So Bjorn got to work on booking an October tour at indoor venues.

That's when the bottom fell out. Not only was I getting lured by these guys at home to come back and be a Nashville sensation, but lawyers from the record label in the States started threatening to put Bjorn out of business if he booked another date for me.

I didn't handle that stress well. I didn't drink again, although it sure would have tasted sweet at that moment, but I fell back into some of the old habits I'd had. Bjorn told me, "Look, I'm working day and night for you. I've talked to you every day since I called and introduced myself. I've almost killed myself with this first tour. I've done everything I can to build your career, not to get rich, but because I believe in you and I love your story. If you want to walk away and go with these guys in America that you don't know, I understand. But I want you to know that I've been here for you, and will be here for you."

I handled that situation poorly. I'd let temptation get the best of me, and let the lure of the big time make me doubt the things and the people who had taken me this far. When Bjorn came back into my bedroom to check on me after he didn't hear from me for a while, he found me eating dinner out of a bucket, just like I had when I'd lived in the culvert.

Not too much longer after that, I wrote a song called "Give It Away" that summed up what it took to keep the real riches in life.

> *If you really want to keep it*
> *You've gotta give it away.*
> *If you really want to help somebody,*

Get on your knees and pray.
If you really want to show the world
Some peace and faith
If you really want to keep it,
Mmm, you gotta give it away.

The October tour got canceled, and I did go back to the States and get in with some friends of Will Kimbrough's who helped book some shows for me in and around Nashville. I played MerleFest, a roots and bluegrass festival in North Carolina. Some of the fans there knew me. Some knew my story. But it was nothing like Sweden. In fact, after my show, the folks who hung around to meet me were Swedes living in America. Some of them had driven hundreds of miles just to see me. That blew my mind. I guess I'd gotten accustomed to fans reacting that way in Sweden, but not in North Carolina or Tennessee. It was like that first night in the Cirkus all over again. My heart was truly full.

I also played *Music City Roots*, a show at a place called the Factory in Franklin, Tennessee, that showcases artists who're devoted to the roots of country and Americana music. I wasn't sure about the categories. I just called it music. My set there got good reviews, and I could sense that the songs, especially "Going Down to the River," continued to touch people.

If I'd let the Devil win those battles in that first year, I never would have been so blessed. During my first trip back home after that initial sweep through Sweden, Emmylou called Babs and invited us over to her house. When I got inside, Emmylou threw her arms around my neck and hugged me like we'd been soul mates for years. It was hard for me to describe to her how much she meant to me back before she knew who I was, back when I was listening to her on a pawnshop record player with nothing but a guitar and a dream. That's not the kind of conversation I know how to have. So I just said, "Darlin', I sure do hope you'll let me sing with you sometime."

She smiled and hugged me again. "You know it," she said. "I can't wait."

———

When I went back to Sweden, me and Jill put out a duet record called *In Tandem*, with a bunch of cover songs that we put a roots twist on. This time I didn't shy away from the press. In fact, I was on a good number of shows. One of them was a talk show called *Nyhetsmorgon*, which translates to *Good Morning, Sweden*. We promoted the new record and sang an old Everly Brothers song called "So Sad to Watch Good Love Gone Bad."

When I got to the television studio, Jill greeted me with the hug that we'd grown accustomed to sharing. Then she looked at me and said, "Doug, you've got food on your wrinkled shirt."

I looked down and said, "Well, whadaya know, I do."

"You didn't look at it or iron it before you put it on?"

I looked at her funny and said, "Why would I do that?"

She mumbled something in Swedish, shook her head, looked back at me, and laughed. "You know we're going on television, right?" she asked.

———

"Yeah," I said. "But people've told me that they love the fact that I'm real." I pointed to my shirt. "This is real. This is me."

We also played a duet of Emmylou's "Boulder to Birmingham," which I'd always thought was one of the most beautiful ballads ever written. We performed that one on television a good bit, including *Live from Eldsjälsgalan*, on TV4 out of Stockholm.

That album went to number one in Sweden too. Two years in a row, I'd been part of a chart-topping record.

———

The band I put together for the second tour was all Swedish except for Babs, who played fiddle with us some. Things didn't work out the way I'd hoped with her managing me, not because she was a bad manager, but because we butted heads over what was important in business and life. My stubborn, independent streak didn't go away when I sobered up and walked in faith. Tell me I have to do something or else, and I'll continue to test to see what you mean. Bjorn stepped back in, as he always did, and I got a lot better at attending meetings and recalling what I needed to do from one day to the next.

As I was assembling the band, a young woman from Estonia named Mai Agan came over and begged to play with me. She'd taken a sixteen-hour boat ride from Estonia to Stockholm to meet me, which caught my attention real quick. Mai was the kind of girl who would have hitchhiked from New York to Austin, or driven from Ithaca to Nashville in a car that didn't look like it'd get out of the driveway. She was a young female version of the good side of me, the side that wasn't partying or ticking people off. Mai played jazz with her own band but loved roots music, and she wanted the experience of touring with me. I thought it was a great idea and told her that the minute I had a sold set of shows, she was on the list.

"When can we play?" she texted me one afternoon.

I texted her back and said I didn't have any gigs at the moment. "I'm just playing on the street," I wrote, which was something I did on an almost daily basis. "You don't want to do that."

Within seconds she texted, "OF COURSE I WANT TO DO THAT!"

So she boated back to Stockholm and the two of us started busking at bus stops and in supermarket parking lots. We'd find sidewalks near concrete walls where the acoustics were good and busk for a couple of hours a day, just like me and Jerry Miller did during my first summer. I bought Mai a small, battery-powered amplifier, and the two of us played wherever we could, always drawing a big crowd.

The shows weren't as numerous and the tour wasn't as hectic as it had been the first time around. But seventy shows in ninety-five days, plus rehearsals and travel and making a stop or two at places like the Norrtälje prison, all of which we squeezed in that first summer, wore me down to a nub. I loved every second of it and wouldn't have traded the experience for anything, but it's not something I wanted to do every day.

People in Sweden were accustomed to me now. They felt like they knew me. And the more comfortable they got with me, the more comfortable I got in sharing my story of redemption.

———

More than once, Swedish friends told me, "Doug, Swedes aren't as religious as Americans. The God talk might turn some people off."

I hoped that wasn't the case, but it didn't matter. I talked about God because God had given me the ability to talk, the mental strength to tell my story, and the gift of being famous enough that people might listen.

People see me as authentic, so I'm obliged to be who I am—a sinner saved by grace and given time to spread God's message of healing through music. There's a whole counter–counter culture thing going on in Sweden now, which has opened up my music and my story to a new audience. The first year, I was the boy band for grandparents, the guy who could fill an arena with people over fifty. But now, kids have done the heavy metal and industrial rock stuff, and they see it commercialized like everything else. So they come around to roots music. That's fine with me. Doesn't matter how they get there. I just want to keep 'em.

A man and his little boy walked by one morning when me and Mai were playing outside a supermarket in Stockholm. The boy recognized me, but the man was in a hurry. I could tell he wasn't listening to me, or to his son. So I broke into John Lennon's "Beautiful Boy." That stopped 'em both cold. The man walked over and listened for a few minutes, his little boy right beside him, holding his arm.

I like to think that dad took a little more time with his son that day.

I like to think I helped.

The crowds at the shows have always been kind to me, but they can be demanding—not in a mean way, but in pushing against you and needing your time. I do my best to give everybody what they want, including a photo and a pat on the back. I give everyone a "God bless you." That's important. I won't stop that, no matter what. One afternoon I got a reminder why. A fella came up. He was covered in tattoos—so many that you didn't know whether to look him in the eye or read him.

He said, "You're Doug Seegers."

And I said, "I am. What can I do for you?"

He said, "I wanted you to know that I just got outta prison, and while I was in, I listened to your song 'Going Down to the River.' It really touched me. I stopped drinking. I believe I'm on the right path."

I hugged that fella for a good long while. It was awfully hard to speak.

During one of me and Mai's subway gigs—the Stockholm subway had great acoustics; turn that amp on and it sounded like a concert hall down there—an American stopped and listened for more than a few minutes, a lot longer than your average subway commuter. He finally said, "Hey, Doug, I really love your music."

The guy gave off a certain vibe, so I asked, "Are you a musician?" I don't know how I knew that, but when you've been an artist all your life, you learn to spot fellow travelers.

He said his name was Fritz and he was the drummer for Jackson Browne's band. One of the oldest and cruelest jokes in the music industry is when you ask an artist to describe his band, he says, "I've got three musicians and a drummer." I didn't share that one with Fritz. I thanked him for stopping to listen, and he said, "We've got a show tonight."

"That's wonderful," I said. "Have a great show."

Mai chatted with the guy a few minutes longer, and it looked like they exchanged phone numbers, which was great. I loved seeing young artists reaching out and networking, something I wish I'd done a better job of when I was young.

After we finished busking in the subway, me and Mai were going back to the hotel when her phone rang. Her eyes got wide when she answered it.

"You're not going to believe this," she said. "Jackson Browne would like for us to come to his show and have dinner with him beforehand."

She looked at me like she was asking permission, so I said, "Well, what are you wearing?"

A little later that evening at the concert hall, Jackson met us at the door. "Doug, I have your record," he said. "I know your story, and I think what you're doing is terrific. Is there any way I could talk you into coming up and doing a song with us during the show?"

That's not an offer you get every day, so I said, "Yeah, sure."

Three hours later, Jackson called me and Mai up onstage where we all performed "Going Down to the River."

I think about that night a fair amount now, because "Going Down to the River" has gotten some age on it. I figure between concerts, sidewalk gigs, television and radio appearances, recording studios, and other places I've been, I've performed that song thousands of times. That's not as many as Jackson's played "Running on Empty" or "Doctor My Eyes." And every night, he sings those songs like it's his first concert.

I understand what Don Henley meant, talking about those last Eagles concerts, when he said he was sick of being "a live jukebox." At times, I have to muster some gumption to play "Going Down to the River." But I do it with every bit of energy I can muster, because I know what it means to people. I know how it's moved people. Yes, it's my thousand-and-first time singing it, but it's the first time somebody in my audience has heard it live. That moment will mean something to 'em. I need to play it with the same emotion and power I had when I sang it for Jill and Magnus outside the Little Pantry That Could. The song is all over YouTube, with people playing covers of it in their bedrooms and even giving guitar lessons on how to find the chords. I need to move the next person who hears it the same way God moved me when I wrote it.

I need to spread the good news. Restoration is out there. You can wash your soul again.

CHAPTER 11

A NEW LANGUAGE

I live in Sweden now. I don't know of any other way to look at it. After my second summer, I stayed because we launched a Christmas album and tour where we played in churches throughout the country. Then I went back to Nashville for a short spell, but came back to Stockholm pretty quick where I worked on two more records and did some more shows.

The Christmas tour really did it for me. Those old churches with their high ceilings and ornate trim; the old craftsman in me studied those buildings and thought about the love and artistry that went into all that work—work that sometimes nobody could see but God. That's enough, I reckon. Things are taking off pretty good. BMG Music, one of the largest music companies in the world, has picked up the publishing and marketing of my records. So I tour between Europe and the States. My story is getting a lot more exposure now, with a new documentary and some possible television spots. It's a high time for a man who's been about as low as you can get.

I'm learning Swedish, picking up as much as I can in conversations and using a computer program to help out. It's slow going. Somebody, I can't remember who, told me that learning a language as an adult is just near impossible. The parts of your brain that do that sorta thing close off after a certain age. I hope that's not true of this. But I'm sure glad it's not true of everything.

I live in the Rootsy house now. Doug's room has become Doug's home, at least for the time being. Bjorn helped me set up a woodshop in a red barn out back of the place. I've built a guitar and a new table. That's where we gather for our daily meetings now. I've got some chairs and a display cabinet coming soon. Nobody has to guess where I am when they show up at the office. You either hear me playing music, struggling through a Swedish vocabulary lesson, or you hear the saws running out back.

Even with the BMG deal and the concerts in America, I gave up the apartment in Nashville, which shocked most of my music friends.

"Nashville's your home," they say, which doesn't strike 'em the least bit funny 'til they think about it for a minute. I tell 'em I can't pay for an apartment that's sitting empty. Bjorn says people do that sort of thing all the time, but I can't see it. Waste isn't in me. I went so long without a home that having one sit empty while I'm five thousand miles away seems almost like a sin.

That doesn't mean I don't go back. I still got my Tennessee driver's license, although I feel like Mr. Magoo when I'm on the road now. When I am in Nashville, I visit Stacy and Becca and I go back to the bridge and see my boys. Some of 'em are still there, still going strong. Others have disappeared. Nobody seems to know where. Nobody but a few of us cares.

I played a show for the Thistle Stop Café not long back. They raised a fair amount. It's a great mission run by saintly people. I also helped produce a record for a girl from Ontario, Canada, named Alexis Taylor. She showed up in Music City with talent, a dream, and not a lot of money. I know that feeling. And I know what can happen if things don't work out right off.

No matter how many shows I play now or how many records I sell around the world, I still think my job is to sound that warning. Be a living example of the worst that can happen to you, as well as the best.

"So, Doug, since you gave up your apartment, where do you stay in Nashville?" People ask that like it's a real question. A man who's lived where I have has no trouble finding a place to lay his head, whether it's under a roof or under the stars.

Jesus told us that no material possession on this earth means anything. And our Savior died naked, without a single thing of this world. His message was pretty simple. It just ain't easy. Love is the greatest thing of all, so give it to everybody, every day.

I've had less than nothing in my life. Now I've had some

hits and hopefully a few more on the way. I've had times when people wouldn't look me in the eye. Now record producers, famous artists, and tour promoters hug me and call me their friend.

I know what it's like to be cast aside, unwanted and unloved. And I know the deep wounds that love can heal.

Love is not the most important thing. It's the only thing.

I try to give as much of it as I can. But I'll never give more than I got.

I dream again now, something I'd forgotten about when I was high. They're glorious dreams. Everybody that's passed through my life's there. Mom, Dad, Googie, Grandma, Dave, Angie—all of 'em. They clap their hands and tap their feet, nodding to the beat and smiling great, young smiles. But I can't hear the music. I know it's there. I know it's beautiful. I strain, but I can't hear a note.

I do so long to hear it. I know I will soon.

I do have a pickup truck that I bought a few years back, the first vehicle I've owned since the car I drove from New York got stolen. Nothing fancy. It's a small two-seater with a camper top on the back.

Just in case.

ACKNOWLEDGMENTS

I would have never thought I'd write a book. Most of my life I would have laughed out loud at the notion of it. I went years without ever reading a book start to finish, so writing one, in my mind, would have been like telling me to go split an atom. I knew it could be done, but I wasn't the fella to do it.

Thankfully, plenty of people came into my life to help me. Not just help with the writing, which was a hard thing, but help me piece together the puzzle of my memory. At times I felt like we were trying to glue together a shattered glass, with shards so small and sharp they'd cut you to the bone. Other times, I wasn't sure it would happen at all; wasn't sure what was left of my old mind could be relied on to tell this story straight. But, as happened too many times for me to count, God put the right people in my life at the right time; people who knew books and how to get the best out of the story of my redemption.

All my songs are stories, little snips of the hard life I've lived and seen and the redemption I've found. This book is just a bigger song, one where the words don't rhyme, but where the feelings are just as raw and real. I have to thank a lot of people for turning my story into something that will hopefully touch many others: The entire management team at Rootsy Music, who believed in me; Bjorn Pettersson and Hakan Olssen for their commitment, hard work, and friendship; Cass Scripps and the entire staff at Agency for Performing Artists (APA) for never losing patience and never giving up on me or my story; my angels, Jill Johnson, John and Penny Combs, Brian Irwin, Magnus Carlsson, Jeff Scarborough, Stacy Downing, Becca Stevens, Charlie Wright, and all the others who showed the love of God in large ways and small when I was living on the streets; my friends Buddy Miller, who I wronged and who forgave me, Will Kimbrough, who believed from the beginning, and the darling Emmylou Harris; all the band members, stage crews, drivers, carpenters, and designers who played with me and did their best to get my message out; all the fans who continue to cheer for me and come to hear me play; literary agent Dan Conaway and everyone at Writer's House who knew how the book industry worked and saw what this project could be before the first word was written; my editor, Webster Younce, and everybody at Thomas Nelson who took a chance on a once homeless musician; my coauthor Steve Eubanks, and to everyone else who contributed to this project in ways big and small, I'll never be able to thank you enough.

I hope what we've done here inspires you. I hope you find God in these pages. He's here, just as he's been with me every day of my life. Good and bad. All you have to do is look.